Tax Secrets of a Real Estate Millionaire

By Dymphna Boholt

A qualified accountant and economist,
Dymphna is regarded as Australia's leading
real estate educator and
tax and asset protection specialist

Tax Secrets of a Real Estate Millionaire

FIRST EDITION 2014

Copyright © 2014 DymphnaBoholt.com

All rights reserved. No part of this publication may be reproduced, stored in a retrieval system, or transmitted in any form or by any means, electronic, mechanical, photocopying, recording or otherwise, without the express written permission from the publisher.

ISBN: 978-1-921225-04-8

Published by DymphnaBoholt.com
PO BOX 944, Buderim, QLD 4556

Email: admin@dymphnaboholt.com
Website: www.iLoveRealEstate.tv
www.DymphnaBoholt.com

Editing by Patti Claridge & Petra Frieser

Project Coordination by Petra Frieser

Printed by Paradigm Print Media

**National Library of Australia
Cataloguing-in-Publication entry**

Boholt, Dymphna.
Tax secrets for real estate millionaires / Dymphna Boholt.
ISBN: 9781921225048 (pbk.).

Real estate investment--Australia.
Real estate investment--Taxation--Australia.
Real property tax--Australia.
Real property and taxation--Australia.

336.220994

Printed in Singapore

Tax Secrets of a Real Estate Millionaire

"I dedicate this book to my late parents Brian and Mary for always instilling in me the belief that I could do anything or be anyone I wanted if I put my mind to it, and to my supportive husband Brian and my beautiful children Justin, Samantha and Luke."

Tax Secrets of a Real Estate Millionaire

Disclaimer

This guide is not intended to be a text on the legal and financial aspects of tax and real estate and should not be relied on as such. No book that is 200 pages or so long can possibly try to set out Australia's tax laws in detail. The Tax Act itself runs to more than a million words and is supported by thousands of rulings and statements from the Tax Office.

Whilst every care has been taken in the preparation of this guide, the publisher will not accept any responsibility or liability for any error however caused, whether by negligence or otherwise in the information contained in it. Readers are urged to seek relevant advice from appropriately qualified professionals for their individual needs.

All figures and statistics recorded in the book are accurate at the time of publishing, however may be subject to change. What we are trying to do, is to acquaint you with the basic thrust of our taxation laws as they apply to real estate investors. If you have an idea of what you must do, and what you can and can't do, you are simply in a much better position when investing, and you will get better results from your taxation professionals.

So keep in mind that many of the statements are only a general guide. If you need specific advice on a specific transaction or event, go see an accountant or tax agent.

Tax Secrets of a Real Estate Millionaire

Special Gift

Free Offer and Resources from Dymphna Boholt

Congratulations! You've come a long way already. If you've read this far then you have distinguished yourself from the rest of the pack and elevated your potential to join the top 5% of the wealth builders on this planet.

I'd like to reward you with ongoing education and free resources so you can continue the momentum that this book has created for you. The value of these resources is well over $985.

Gift #1: The Ultimate 1 Day Real Estate Success Seminar. Spend a whole day with me and I will reveal to you my unique real estate secrets quadrant which is protect, maximise, wealth, cash flow. Some teach one or two of the secrets but nobody teaches all four and how important they are in growing your wealth fast.
Value $495, Yours Free!

Gift #2: Bring a second person to ultimate real estate secrets of event for free.
Value $295, Yours Free!

Gift #3: Online audio newsletter, The Property Prophet Report. Every week I keep you updated with my audio newsletter. The property market is always changing, get the inside knowledge and the unfair advantage on how to capitalise regardless of the economic climate.
Value $195, Yours Free!

To qualify for the bonuses, you need to register at the following exclusive link:

http://realestatesuccess.com.au/985bonus

Tax Secrets of a Real Estate Millionaire

Table of Contents

	Page

Chapter one — 9
Be tax smart, not tax ignorant, being tax smart, saves you money, being tax ignorant, costs you money
Why is Real Estate so tax efficient?... Tax Efficiency Ranking... Make the Tax Man your business partner!... Exclude, Deduct, Defer and Convert.

Chapter two — 19
Turn your lifestyle into a business, make your lifestyle tax-deductible
Treat your property like a business... Increase your Property Income... Reduce your property expenses... Getting the right loan.

Chapter three — 31
Structure for maximum tax efficiency
What structures are available?... Owning property in individual names... Owning property in a company name... Owning property in a trust name... Putting a tax effective structure together.

Chapter four — 52
Negative gearing exposed
Is buying negatively cash flowed property wrong?... Take the emotion out of investing... Create a plan... Paper losses.

Chapter five — 64
Negative gearing nuances
Negative gearing through a hybrid trust... A big fat warning!... Other areas of concern.

Chapter six — 72
The flipside, positive gearing
Positive? Negative? How will I know?

Chapter seven — 86
Maximise your tax strategy
Use tax-deductions to generate real estate cash flow... What types of real estate maximise tax-free income?... Depreciation and effective life tables... Calculating deductions... Diminishing Value Method... Prime Cost Method... Effective life of a depreciating asset... Decline in value of a depreciating asset... Which method of depreciation should we use?

Chapter eight   95
Getting cash credits for tax on real estate up front
Income Tax Variations... So what is rental property income anyway?... Rental property income classifications... Non-income receipts... One off tax credit variations.

Chapter nine   101
Tax-free wealth creation
Your principal place of residence... The dangers of trading in your principal place of residence.

Chapter ten   108
Investor versus trader
Investor... Trader / dealer... Wrapping... What type of person do wraps suit?... Possible wrap outcomes... Types of wraps... Trader / dealer expenses... Car expenses and substantiation... Cents per km method... 12% of original value method... 1/3 of actual expenses method... Log book method... Home office expenses... Claiming the cost of travel expenses... Travelling deductions being wasted!!!... Travel Allowances versus Travel Expenses... Verification... Tax returns.

Chapter eleven   131
The Tax that gets you when you sell!
Capital gains and real estate... Two methods for calculating Capital Gains Tax... Essential Capital Gains Tax tips.

Chapter twelve   143
The hidden killer - GST!
Residential Rents... What does the Tax Office mean by new residential premises?... So who has to be registered for GST?... Commercial Premises... I have made a mistake!

Chapter thirteen   154
Deductions that maximise your profit and cut the cost of tax

Chapter fourteen   164
Finance, making the most of borrowed money
Purpose of the funds test... One little legal loophole... Not the best strategy!... So, what should John and Edith have done?... Converting bad debt into good debt... Smart money flow... Loan Splitting... Offset accounts.

Chapter fifteen   182
Family arrangements, investing with children
Shared equity ownership... First home owner's grant... Who can apply for the first home owner's grant?... Renting your way through uni... Investing income for children... Children's earned income... Divorce.

Chapter sixteen   192
Succession planning
What happens if you inherit?... So what is a Will?... Enduring Power of Attorney... What renders a Will invalid?... Testamentary trusts... Inherited property.

Chapter seventeen   202
Investing overseas
Tax scams and tax havens... Overseas investments and Capital Gains Tax...

Chapter eighteen   210
Planning for retirement
Superannuation... Tax offsets... Co-contributions... Self-managed fund contribution limits... Self-managed versus managed... Borrowing in super funds... In specie transfers... Nearing retirement... Life insurance policies.

Chapter nineteen   224
What to do at the end of the financial year; record keeping
The end of the financial year... Visiting your accountant... Interim visits to your accountant... Asset and ownership registers... Assessment checklist... Tax audits... What do you do if the tax auditor wants to come and visit?... Record Keeping tips... Personal Records Chart... Cash Flow Analysis Chart... Checklist of Rental Property Deductions Chart... Investing Entity Tax Return checklist.

Appendix a - Summary of GST Status   237
Appendix b - Trust Capital Gains Tax Rates   238
Appendix c - Effective Life Table   239
Appendix d - Capital Works Table   249
Appendix e - Indexation Tables   251
Appendix f - History of Tax Law   253
Appendix g - Tax Rates   260
Appendix h - Real Estate Purchase Expenses   262
Appendix i - Summary of Car Expense Methods   263
Appendix j – Travel Claims within Australia reasonable limits   264
Appendix k – Countries Australia has a tax treaty with   268

Chapter 1

Be tax smart, not tax ignorant
Being tax smart, saves you money
Being tax ignorant, costs you money

For many Australians, the word taxation sends bolts of either fear or outrage running through their bodies. It's a simple fact however, that without some form of community collections process, any civilised society would not be able to build or maintain the infrastructure necessary to support civilised living. By this, I mean it is the taxation system which pays for roads, schools, hospitals, defence and all common community facilities.

I do agree however, that our current taxation system is cumbersome, archaic, Draconian, unfair and downright confusing. I have very strong beliefs as to what reforms should be undertaken to our taxation system which would simplify it enormously, do away with a lot of red tape and bureaucracy, as well as the need for many accountancy offices, but that's a whole other story.

Over the last two hundred years taxation has become the norm, an accepted fact of life. The first tax introduced in Australia was an import duty which was imposed to raise money to build a gaol and an orphanage in Sydney in 1805. In fact, when you look up the history books, you will find the taxes levied for most of the 1800's in Australia were mainly death duties, land taxes and liquor and tobacco taxes. This gives you a little of an insight into what was of greatest concern back then!

It's actually interesting to relate what was happening in our Australian history to the actions, or should I say 're-actions', of the Government of the time, to the types of taxes they decided to impose. For instance, in the 1800's, the nation was getting established, and the main form of taxing came from ownership of land in the form of Land Tax. Then, I guess, because they figured there would be less complaint, Death Duty was imposed on the assets you owned when you died.

Then, when the economy seemed to be having a bit of an upward surge due to the large production and sale of liquor and tobacco, what happens? "Oh, I think we should have a liquor and tobacco tax." A Liquor Tax of 10 shillings a gallon was introduced.

As gold started to become the big wealth creation strategy in the mid 1800's, what do the powers that be decide? "The peasants are getting a bit too rich, we should introduce a gold tax". Then, as our early entrepreneurs started to implement manufactured growth strategies such as subdividing and selling off parcels of their land, you guessed it, a Land Tax on subdivisions was introduced in 1877.

Tasmania was the first state to introduce an Income Tax in 1880, with other states following suit over the next 20 years. However, it wasn't until 1915 that a national Income Tax was constituted and the Tax Office was renamed from the Land Tax Office to the Australian Taxation Office (ATO). That was less than one hundred years ago.

In 1916, the government of the day obviously thought the post World War I population was having far too much fun when it introduced an entertainment tax! Then in 1918 a 1/2d (halfpenny) war tax was levied on postage stamps but was then repealed in 1920, but the increase in postage remained. By 1930, the first Sales Tax was introduced at 2.5% to offset the fall in customs revenues.

1941 saw the introduction of a war tax on payroll (Payroll Tax) to pay for child endowment. However, with the stress of World War II taking its toll and many of our diggers not returning from fighting abroad, much of their property and assets were transferred to family and loved ones before they headed off to war. So of course the Government was missing out on its precious Death Duty – can't have that now can we? You guessed it; in 1941 a Gift Tax was legislated.

In 1944, the end of the war saw returned soldiers coming back to Australia and either entering business or working for Government and private companies, so a uniform pay as you earn or PAYE (now known as PAYG or Pay As You Go) was introduced. So that business owners didn't escape the tax detector, a provisional tax was also introduced. This fitted in nicely, as the onus to collect the tax was placed on the employer and not the dreaded tax collector.

> "complacency is threatening life as we know it in Australia"

You can see what was happening over all these years – it's like having a spoilt child. If you let them get away with something once, they just keep pushing the boundaries further and further until something snaps. As a nation, we have been conditioned to accept the tax regime and our complacency is to blame.

When I teach real estate wealth creation strategies, I call it the 'comfy couch syndrome' and believe me, it is a very dangerous place to be. Inaction, indecision and complacency are threatening the future of our life in Australia as we know it.

The years roll by, each government, regardless of political persuasion, adding their own set of additional taxes, changes and complications. 1984 to 1986 were big years with the introduction of the Medicare Levy (just a new name for the same old tax), Capital Gains Taxes and Fringe Benefit Taxes.

With Income Taxes being at saturation point, we then got really ingenious and implemented another tax called the 'Goods and Services Tax' (GST) in 2000 to celebrate the new millennium and once again the onus of collection fell in the hands of the business owners. It was supposed to be a trade off against the abolition of all other incidental taxes like Stamp Duty, Land Tax and Sales Tax, but one woman's complaining about GST on milk and bread left us with most of the incidental taxes remaining like Stamp Duty and Land Tax – but no GST on milk and bread! Ironic don't you think?

Of course, the latest industries to be targeted are the mining industry and carbon emissions industries. Whenever something becomes popular or profitable, it becomes the target for a new "must have" tax. Yet again history repeats itself.

For those of you who have a need for more background information on the history of our tax system, a more comprehensive time line of the history of taxation can be found at Appendix F[1].

Is it interesting though, to see just how much over the years, we have allowed our Governments to tamper with the tax system

---

[1] Parliamentary Library *History of Tax Law*

and it is 'us', the voting majority, who are responsible for allowing Australia to become one of the most highly taxed countries in the Western world. Our tax system has become a pawn for electoral manipulation, treasury power plays, and to alleviate the boredom of government bureaucrats; "Let's see how much we can mess around with the superannuation laws this week!"

Perhaps I am being a little cynical. However, it is ridiculous to the point of being comical, when you look at the tax laws and all the budget changes that have taken place over the years, and how this has affected tax law and made inconspicuous dates like 19 September 1985 so important. That was the date Capital Gains Tax was introduced and anything purchased before that date is exempt from Capital Gains Tax and anything purchased after that date is now subject to tax on the profit when sold. Don't even get me started on all the dates for superannuation or depreciation!

Regardless of your political views or knowledge of our taxation system, you must agree that some form of taxing, whether income or consumer based, needs to be in place to pay for all the common infrastructure and social support mechanisms that we enjoy as part of our everyday life. As individuals, we have to deal with the laws of the land as they are legislated at this point in time. So as intelligent, astute taxpayers, it is our responsibility to learn as much as we possibly can about what we can and can't do, so that we can maximise our 'after tax' profits.

> "Focus on earning the money first and then be as efficient as possible in paying your tax"

That means learning the legal loop holes and strategies that can literally save you thousands of dollars in wasted, unnecessary taxes.

Tax Secrets of a Real Estate Millionaire

Being tax smart can dramatically increase your investment returns. How many times have you wished you knew something about a law or tax model before you took action on a particular deal or investment?

The purpose of this book is to alert you to the potential pitfalls, as well as your potential tax procedures, to increase your bottom line returns, resulting from the tax phenomenon. Obviously, tax changes occur over time and even though at the time of writing, the facts and suggestions included in this book are accurate - changes in legislation may have altered, and this may affect your outcome. Additionally, your particular situation may require a slightly different strategy to maximise your desired outcome. This is why I always highly recommend you discuss your situation with an accountant who specialises in accounting for property investors, and who can assist you with your particular needs.

Why is real estate so tax efficient?

When you compare real estate investing with other forms of investment, it certainly holds its own on the tax efficiency stakes. Even against some of the more recognised tax schemes, when you look at the end result, including income growth after tax, I believe real estate is still the overall winner.

Let's have a quick look at some of these.

Tax efficiency ranking

Real Estate versus Cash?

Clearly here, there isn't even any competition. Real estate wins every time. The deductibility of related expenses, including interest on borrowings, is the same for both investment types. However, the benefit of being able to claim a tax-deduction for the depreciating value of building, fixtures and fittings, even after claw backs on sale, still puts real estate streets above any cash competitor.

Real Estate versus Shares?

This is a more controversial one. The stock market lovers will argue that the higher potential growth in the stock market will outweigh the small additional benefit of having part of your income tax-free, as a result of depreciation deductions. The real estate enthusiasts on the other hand, will argue the income returns are higher and the growth returns are comparable without the degree of risk the stock market poses, and the tax efficiency of the depreciation deductions far outweigh any franking tax credit benefits. As an accountant and economist, I can see both sides, but as an avid real estate investor I am definitely biased.

Real Estate versus Business?

This question is more a question of how long is a piece of string. Business is such a wide category and covers everything from the corner store, network marketing businesses and internet businesses to multi-national corporations. In general, businesses certainly do have the capacity to be very tax efficient when structured correctly – but that's a topic for another time.

Real Estate versus Special Tax Schemes?

I thought I should touch on the multitude of tax based investments and schemes that are promoted every year around the end of the financial year. They range in nature from forestry to fish farms, to share warrants, and many others. The basic concept is that taxpayers usually borrow to invest, using their home as security, pay a year's interest upfront, and claim a tax-deduction in that year directly against their other income.

Over the ensuing years, they usually cost in ongoing fees and interest which is tax-deductible with a vain hope that a profit will be made at some point in time in the future. The trouble is most never make a profit in the future.

Tax Secrets of a Real Estate Millionaire

Check out the Australian Security and Investment Commission's website for a more comprehensive discussion: www.moneysmart.gov.au

I believe even the legitimate ones don't stack up to the income, growth and tax effectiveness of real estate, particularly when you take into account the benefits of using leverage to compound your result. But remember – I'm biased!

Real estate is up there as one of the most tax efficient investments, so what else do we need to know about being an efficient real estate investor?

The first thing is to get your head around working <u>with</u> the Tax Office, regardless of whether you agree with the law or not.

Make the tax man your business partner!

If you think of the Tax Office as your business partner - and yes, I know that may sound absurd to some of you - and the tax law as the terms and conditions of the partnership agreement, then paying tax is nothing more than the distribution of profits in accordance with your partnership agreement. A novel concept don't you think?

The tax man is also your business finance partner if you own a business or property. The tax man allows you to use all the income you collect for a period of time, usually anywhere from three months to up to eighteen months, without requiring his/her share of profits. This is a form of interest-free financing.

Now that we have recognised the tax man as a friendly and not a hostile enemy, it is easier for us to deal with maximising legitimate deductions which are integral to the investment or business we are running, and increase the bottom-line profits and the long-term benefit of all parties concerned. Effectively, you are profit sharing with the Tax Office. The more skilled and knowledgeable you are on the tax laws, the less your profit sharing arrangement with the tax man is likely to be.

So how does this work?

Exclude, Deduct, Defer and Convert

These are the four key concepts in tax planning, that reduce the profit sharing agreement you have with your new business partner and financier - that is, the Tax Office.

Exclude

Profits made on certain assets are exempt from Income Tax and Capital Gains Tax. In New Zealand, these types of assets include most real estate. In Australia, it is limited to your home or 'principal place of residence' (PPR). Maximising capital growth on your principal place of residence is a great way to gain wealth without having to pay tax.

Deduct

Learn the art of thinking like a business owner. Running your activities like a business can slash thousands of dollars off your profit share arrangement or tax bill. Many expenses are costs that we would incur in our everyday living and investing, but may well be tax-deductible if we can relate the expenditure to the income being earned.

Defer

Laws exist to allow you to postpone or defer your tax or profit sharing arrangement until a later date. In this way, the Tax Office is acting as a financier to you until you decide to sell your property, at which time an adjustment is made for the previous year's tax credits. This phenomenon is called depreciation.

It is a tax-deduction for not spending any money. It is a tax-deduction for the estimated decrease in value of part or all of the real estate purchase.

Tax Secrets of a Real Estate Millionaire

Convert

This is the process of having profits counted as capital profits, and therefore taxed concessionally, rather than income profits where the Tax Office shares in the profits at a much greater percentage.

Chapter 2

Turn your lifestyle into a business
Make your lifestyle tax-deductible

The true secret of saving money on your tax bill, is being able to deduct expenditure that you have incurred anyway, before you pay your tax. It's a simple little formula, but it can mean big dollars in tax savings if you structure yourself for tax savings.

Step One:	Earn your income
Step Two:	Pay your expenses
Step Three:	Pay tax on the balance

Unfortunately, there are too many taxpayers – namely those who work for someone else (a boss), who pay tax this way.

Tax Secrets of a Real Estate Millionaire

- Earn income
- Pay tax
- Pay expenses out of balance

When you start to turn your lifestyle into a business, you are converting what would have previously been non-deductible expenditure paid out of after-tax dollars, into tax-deductible expenditure paid out of pre-tax dollars. Let me give you some examples to show you how this works:-

---

Example:

A friend of mine worked in a government job and longed to own a boat; not just a boat but a catamaran. He could never justify such a big expense to either himself or his wife, until he started to do some calculations on what would happen if he turned the purchase into a business.

By making the boat a business asset and putting it to work to earn income by hiring the boat out to charter with a recognised boat charter company, it meant all his expenses relating to the boat including interest on the loan, insurance, repairs and travel to conduct maintenance checks and repairs, were now tax-deductible against the income earned from chartering the boat.

Of course, he needed to keep track of the amount of time he spent using the boat himself for private purposes and that percentage of the total expenses would not be tax-deductible. So if he used the boat two months of the year himself for holidaying etc. then two twelfths or one sixth of the total expenses he would not be able to claim. He was going to buy a boat anyway – this way the income it earns helps him pay for it and he can claim the expenses as a tax-deduction.

The laws on having boats and aeroplanes as businesses has changed over the years so make sure you check the current tax rules before rushing out and buying either.

While my mate was fixated on a boat – it could just as easily have been a holiday apartment, luxury car, aeroplane or rural property. What you are actually doing, is converting a lifestyle choice into a business decision.

Example:

Having grown up on a cattle property, my love for the land has always been very strong, so I put my money where my mouth was, when an opportunity came up to buy my 54 acre piece of paradise. I call it my toy farm because it is a lot smaller than the properties I grew up on.

Whilst I wanted to have the lifestyle, I knew how much work even a toy farm would be. For this reason, initially I set it up to be commercially viable, so that I could have the lifestyle I wanted without the work. I set up a commercially viable hydroponics operation growing predominantly lettuces. The income from the farm was sufficient to pay for a fulltime farm manager to maintain the property and keep it looking beautiful.

My motives were not purely financially driven, but also lifestyle driven. Having said that, not only did the commercially viable hydroponics operation mean I got my farm maintained for free from a tax perspective, it also had a flow on effect in terms of cars and machinery which then also become a business expense, and therefore tax-deductible.

Another example:

If somebody liked doing craft and that was their passion, a perfect example of making their lifestyle tax-deductible is to make their craft profitable. I have lots of clients doing exactly that, whether it be craft, painting, scrapbooking, or any other hobby that is their love. So why not make the expenditure that you would have had anyway, tax-deductible or even better than that, make it profitable.

Tax Secrets of a Real Estate Millionaire

Some obvious ways to do exactly that are to set up an avenue to sell your finished product. The more traditional ways of doing that would be the local craft market, CWA drives, or even offer them to retailers to onsell. However, with the advance of modern technology, the profitability of a home-based business can be taken to a whole other level.

> ## Example:
> One of my clients had a passion for craft; scrapbooking, patchwork and generally making pretty things.
>
> She set up her own website through one of the free web providers, took some pictures of her work, and loaded them onto her website. She set up a blog page and showed views of how the finished items were actually made. The idea took off and now she has a thriving home-based business, that is not only profitable, but all the things that she used to spend money on anyway, are now tax-deductible.

If we take all of this to another level, once you have a profitable endeavour running from a premises, it also means that home office expenses become deductible. This could mean that a percentage of your mortgage interest, electricity and rates could all be tax-deductible.

The downside of claiming these expenses is that when you sell your home, a percentage of your capital gain, will as a consequence, be taxable (See Chapter 11 on Capital Gains Tax).

> ## Example:
> My sister is in a similar situation. She is a teacher, but her real passion through all these years is painting. After an illness and some major life changes, she made the conscious decision to follow her passion.

cont'd

Initially she went through the rollercoaster ride, as many artisans do, of wondering if anyone will actually like what she creates. So she put some of her paintings up for sale on the internet on 'eBay' and bingo, people want them and are prepared to pay for them.

Her passion is 'yard art', painting pictures for the outdoors and multi-media paintings for the indoors. She now has her own website and blog page and as a result, gets to buy her paint, canvas, brushes and any other ancillary items out of pre-tax dollars.

As you can see, by setting up profit centres around your lifestyle decisions, you can not only have the lifestyle you want, but make your lifestyle tax-deductible at the same time. Turning your lifestyle decision into a business, a commercially viable business, gives your endeavours longevity and sustainability.

I remember advising a would-be charity organisation about this concept, and their retort was that they had very large pockets and didn't need to make a profit.

" profitability guarantees sustainability"

My response was clear: "No matter how big your pockets are, if you are not topping them up, they will eventually run dry."

This concept can be taken further when you consider turning your passion into an income source and ultimately into your primary source of income. After all, isn't that the ultimate? Earning an income doing what you love? That way it's not work, and you are earning money doing it.

There are rules around how much money your need to make and how much you have invested into the business which affect whether the Tax Office sees it as a business or meanly a hobby, so make sure you talk to your accountant about this for your particular area of interest or passion.

When you add the benefits of earning your income as a business and being able to earn that income through tax efficient structures such as discretionary and hybrid trusts, the prospect of following your passion and actually making a living from it, becomes very attractive.

I deal with this concept in more detail in the next chapter, and for even more information about how tax and trusts work and the best ways to use them for asset protection visit my websites:

WWW.ILoveRealEstate.tv and www.DymphnaBoholt.com

Treat your property like a business

You need to treat your property investment purchase as you would a business. It is crucial that you understand this in order to develop a successful investment portfolio. I am going to propose two things here:

- every property purchase should be selected on its merits;
- every purchase needs to be a **business** decision.

In viewing your property as a business, one of the very first things you need to do is to analyse your goals. What do you want to achieve over the next few years? What position do you want to be in, in five years' time? Having made those very important goals very clear, you then need to determine the strategies you need to put in place in order to achieve them.

When you buy your property as a **business transaction** your mindset changes. Your logic kicks into gear, and your emotion takes a back step, which it should. What I have found is that if someone is buying a business, they'll recognise, "This is new for me. I need to talk to my accountant about how to buy this business and what tax structure to put it in for both asset protection and taxation reasons." That approach is normal, appropriate and wise.

My suggestion is that you approach the purchase of your investment property and taxation in the same way. For instance, talk to a suitably qualified accountant that specialises in property purchases, and in particular, asset protection. Look at the property on a profit and loss basis.

Believe me, many people have trouble actually working that out. The structure in which your business is purchased is crucial. The way ownership of a particular property is held, will affect the amount of tax that you will pay on a property.

Increase your property income

A profit in a business is what's left over after expenses are deducted from income. Well, it's no different in an investment property purchase. You have the rental income coming in, minus expenses such as loan repayments and repairs. This is the area in your business plan where you consider such

> " property should be looked at on a profit and loss basis"

things as how you can increase your rental income and therefore your profit.

When you have a shop or other business, you are constantly thinking about what else you can do and how you can give better service, so you can increase your turnover. How much extra income would you generate by adding a slush-puppy machine, or a new line of soda? In a rental property, extra income means catering for your tenants in a better way.

There might be ways in which you can invest a relatively small amount of money for a relatively larger gain. It is all about value-adding. Just like at McDonald's: "Do you want fries and a drink with your order?" For your tenant it might be: "Would air-conditioning make you happier, stay longer and pay more rent?"

The extra things you do, and the extra services you provide can make all the difference to your rental property business, your bottomline profit and the overall growth of your investment portfolio. As an astute investor, you would always be considering ways to increase your property business profit. Here are a few questions that you might ask about an investment property you are considering buying, or about a property you already own to help maximise bottom line profits.

What can I do to make this property more profitable?

- Can I create a storage facility somewhere?
- Can I convert this into a dual income property?
- If I added a carport, would that increase my return?
- Would adding airconditioning make a difference to my yield? How much would airconditioning cost me?
- Should I offer furniture or internet connections?
- How can I make this property more desirable to my tenants overall and thus be justified in charging more rent?

Every time you put your hand in your pocket to spend money on a property, you need to ask yourself: "What is my return on that investment?" In the example following, it is well worth my while to spend the $700 and get the extra $1,300 per annum return. Unfortunately, when talking about an investment property, people tend to draw a blank, or their logical hat gets blown out the window and they don't think of their property purchase like a business purchase.

Example:

I was considering updating one of my rental units recently. It is in a block of four units and I wanted to bring it on a par with the other units. The tenant was moving out after 10 years, and the unit was run down.

Because the block of units is located in a warm climate, I asked the agent about providing airconditioning and by how much I would be able to increase the rent if I did install a $700 air-conditioner. The agent informed me that air-conditioning would increase the rent by about $25 per week. Multiplying $25 per week by 52 weeks, I arrived at $1,300. A $1,300 return on a $700 investment. That's approximately a 185% return per annum! Needless to say, I installed an air-conditioning unit!

Reduce your property expenses

When you have a shop, you are also always trying to find ways to reduce your expenses. I was having a chat recently to a cabinetmaker who was looking at purchasing a particular machine, which was fairly expensive. I asked him what he thought was the added advantage in having this machine. In other words, how was having this machine going to add value and extra profit to the business?

For one thing, the cabinetmaker told me, it would save him two men's wages per year, because the machine had the capacity to do what the men were currently doing. In addition, he could then use those two men to go out and do more installing and other related tasks, in order to increase the business's bottom line. In my opinion, that cabinetmaker made a wise business decision.

It's exactly the same with your property. Ask yourself, "How can I reduce my expenses to increase my bottomline?" "Do I need to spend money in order to save money in the long term?" "Am I being inefficient with the expenses on my property, and could costs be cut without compromising quality?"

Here are some ideas you might like to consider for your new purchase or existing investment property:

- Negotiate management terms with your managing agent. Management rates and terms are flexible and the more competitive the market, the lower the negotiations can go. Also, the more properties you have in an area, the better the deal you are likely to be able to negotiate.

- Always pay your rates on time as councils impose a penalty if you don't pay your rates by a set date.

- Have your rates reassessed! In some areas, rates are just automatically increased, and I have known of a number of cases where asking for a rates assessment review resulted in the rates bill coming down, even if only marginally.

- Shop around when getting maintenance carried out on your property. Your agent could be getting complacent about getting you the best deal on cost of repairs and in some cases, they may be taking a cut or a referral fee for giving the work to a particular handyman or contractor.

- Shop around for the right insurance policy. Whilst premiums vary greatly, the cheapest one may not always be the best option. Make sure you are adequately covered in the areas you need cover.

- Consider including some or all of the outgoings on your rental property in the lease, so the tenant is responsible for the costs. Whilst this is usually not popular in the residential market, it is common in the commercial market.

Tax Secrets of a Real Estate Millionaire

- One of the areas where you can really cut costs is having the right loan. Over the years I have seen many clients wasting sometimes hundreds of dollars every month by having badly structured loans. Cash flow is the life blood of any business, and your investment property is a business.

Since a correctly structured loan makes such a difference to the profitability of your real estate investment, I thought we should focus on some of the more important issues about financing and structuring your loan.

Getting the right loan

When purchasing a business, you would normally do a substantial amount of research on what you are able to borrow at any point in time on that business. You would research the serviceability on that business. You would research the financing limitations on that business. Conversely, when people buy investment properties, they normally just go to their regular banker or broker and say, "Can I get a loan to buy this property?" However, what is really sad, is that in most cases, provided the client meets the bank's or financier's criteria, the answer is "Sure, sign here, press hard - three copies."

This happens all the time without any consideration for cross securitisation, cash flow, taxation implication, structure or the client's future purchasing intentions or capabilities. A badly structured loan can really limit your long-term goals.

It is this type of incompetence that encouraged me to set up my own mortgage brokering franchise, and I encourage you to contact them for a free financial fitness health check at **www.investorloansnetwork.com.au**

Example:

A couple decide they want to buy a positively cash flowed property, and in their searching, they find a nice little over-50s retirement duplex and/or unit. Unbeknown to our investing couple, borrowing on this type of property would probably be restricted to a maximum of 60% LVR (Loan to Value Ratio). Furthermore, in some cases, when the units are small – less than 50 square metres, such as hotel rooms and small bedsits, the borrowing levels could even be lower or non-existent.

Our couple is equity-rich, but they have been persuaded to buy this particular property because their friend bought one and everyone says it is a great idea. Their friendly bank loans officer says there won't be a problem with borrowing. What the bank officer is not telling them is that they will be taking a big chunk of their available equity in their home in order to buy the property and the two loans would be cross securitised.

They might be better to *not* buy that type of property, because it requires so much of their available equity, thereby limiting their available equity for future purchases. Also, the bank would have complete control, with security over both properties! What they should have done, is take control of their borrowing destiny, and not have their investment portfolio tied up in the same bank as the home loan on their existing property. The type of property they should have selected, because they had limited equity/funds available for investment from their existing assets, should have been a property on which they could have borrowed more than 60%.

Chapter 3

Structure for maximum tax efficiency

What do I mean by structuring for maximum tax efficiency?

I mean owning your asset or property in the name of the legal entity which will pay the least amount of tax, both now and in the future. Many investors take a very short term view when it comes to reducing their tax and often only think about how much tax they will be saving on their next tax return. They should be taking into account how long they intend to own the property, their reasons for purchasing the property, and how the purchase fits into their overall investment goals.

Let me explain further.

Tax Secrets of a Real Estate Millionaire

The most efficient way to earn income, and pay less tax, is to even out the family income amongst the adults, and pay the children as much as they are entitled to as either earned or unearned income. This means, in an ideal situation, the adults would earn exactly the same amount, and children able to work (at least part-time after school and on weekends), would earn an amount proportionate to their earning capacity. Children too young to work would earn unearned income of $416. This figure used to be higher when children could claim the low income offset rebate, however, this was abolished in mid 2010. Using up the children's unearned tax-free threshold can be done by either setting up investments such as term deposits in the children's name that would earn about that amount of income for the year, or giving them a distribution from trust income.

This process is called 'using the lowest common denominator'.

When the family income comes from a business, utilising the income distribution process of the lowest common denominator is relatively easy. Typically, the business would be run through a family discretionary trust or a hybrid trust with a corporate trustee (I will explain the rationale for this later), and through a process of paying wages to family members and distribution of profits, the family income can be easily evenly distributed. Care of course must be taken to comply with the personal services legislation.

The process of evening out the family income is obviously much harder when the adults in the family earn their income from salary and wages, where earnings are fixed, and quite often very disproportionate. Clearly, simple things like putting term deposits and cash investments in the lower income earner's name all help to even out the income. Even investing the family share portfolio or managed funds in the lower income earner's name all makes good sense. But what about property or even a share portfolio that is geared (by this I mean, borrowed money invested in the share market)?

Well, this is where the tax question starts to become complicated. Many investors choose to invest in negatively geared investments in the highest income earner's name so that any tax losses resulting from the investment can be claimed as a tax-deduction against their salary or wage. Whilst this strategy may render a short-term tax benefit to the taxpayer, it will pose a tax problem for the taxpayer a few years down the track when the property (or share portfolio to a lesser extent) is no longer negatively geared, or when the property or share portfolio is sold and a capital gain is made. The additional positive cash flow or capital gain would then be taxed at the higher income earner's tax rate!

So what is the answer? To answer this properly I want to make sure you understand the full implications of what it means to invest in either individual names or in the name of a company or trust, as the ramifications are much broader than just tax.

What structures are available?

Owning property in individual names

The simplest and most obvious way to own/hold assets is in individual names. The problem is that not only do you leave yourself open to litigation, but also any income you receive from that asset is added to the income you earn from your salary or wage and may push you into a higher tax bracket. This may result in you paying more tax than would otherwise be necessary, if you were structured correctly.

Conversely, there may be significant tax advantages through negative gearing etc., that you could be giving up for the sake of asset protection if you choose to hold negatively geared investments in structures rather than in your individual names. This is particularly the case for those who earn their primary income as an individual.

There are other ways to have your cake and eat it too when it comes to negative gearing. By this I mean owning your asset in a structure name, thus protecting it for asset protection purposes and having the tax benefit of flexibility to distribute cash flow profit and more importantly, capital gains profits to the lowest income earner, but I will explain that later.

Owning property in a company name

I am constantly astounded at the number of people who go and buy appreciating assets such as real estate in a company structure and when pressed as to why a company structure was used as opposed to any other structure, the answer varies from asset protection, to, "I thought there would be more tax-deductible expenses," to "Because the next door neighbour said I should." All these reasons are **flawed**.

Companies are great structures to act as a separate legal entity and are useful as part of an asset protection system. They are even a great vehicle to use as part of a tax reduction system, but simply owning real estate, which is an appreciating asset, in a company structure, provides few of these benefits and means you are going to pay more tax in the long run.

Why is that? Let me explain:

If an investment property is bought in your own name, in a super fund's name or even in a trust structure's name, and you sell it, you are entitled to a 50% Capital Gains Tax exemption. However, when you buy the same investment property in a company structure, no such Capital Gains Tax exemption is available. This means that you will pay **double** the amount of tax for no reason!

I remember reading an article in the Financial Review that was reporting on a luncheon held in Sydney where there was a prominent barrister who was a tax and asset protection speaker, speaking alongside a taxation department representative. One of the discussions to come from the debate was that the Tax Office representative believed the sole purpose for owning assets in trust and company structures was to avoid or minimise tax, whereas the barrister argued both were used primarily for asset protection rather than tax. However, what was more intriguing about the article, was that the barrister was speaking about a common practice of using negatively geared investment properties to reduce tax for small business owners.

He cited a case of a profitable small business which conducted its business directly in a company structure and every time they felt their profits were up and taxes needed to be reduced, they bought another negatively geared investment property. Of course, in order to get the tax-deduction, because their business was working directly out of the company, investment properties had to be purchased in the company name as well.

In the long term, this not only caused a problem for asset protection, but it also created an ever-increasing unnecessary tax liability when the properties were sold, as the Capital Gains Tax payable on the sale of the properties would be double what they needed to be.

Companies can still be very useful structures when combined with other entities. However, we first need to understand the uses and implications of the other available structures.

Owning property in a trust name

Now let's take a look at a little more complex method of owning assets, protecting them, and having the flexibility to always distribute income and capital gains to the lowest common denominator.

The fundamental concept behind the use of trusts has not really changed very much since medieval times. Basically, a trust is a deed, or a book of rules, that sets out the rights and obligations of all the parties. There are a number of important roles described in the trust deed that carry out these rights and obligations. The main participants in a trust are the 'trustee' and the 'beneficiaries'.

The **trustee** is appointed to look after the assets and income, and distribute them according to the rules outlined in the trust deed. The trustee can be an individual, or more commonly for asset protection reasons, the trustee is most often a company.

The **beneficiaries** are the collective of ultimate owners of the assets of the trust and are the ones that receive any income and capital distributions from the trust. Depending on how the trust is written, the trust deed may allow for different classes of beneficiaries who are entitled to different classes of either income or capital. These types of trusts are particularly useful as entities that have fixed ownership, but may have the ability to distribute income to other nominated beneficiaries.

Two other positions which have responsibilities to the trust and its beneficiaries are the 'settlor' and the 'appointor', sometimes called guardian, 'grantor' or 'protector'.

The **settlor** can be anyone, but is usually the solicitor or accountant who has created the trust deed for you, and is required to sign or execute the trust deed. The settlor is also the person who feeds in gifts, or donates the initial assets of the trust. These initial assets of the trust are usually just a nominal value such as $10 to $20. Be aware that this is a gift – it cannot then be billed to you as part of the setting up of the trust.

The **appointor**, also known as the **guardian** or the **protector**, in most trust deeds, is given the onerous responsibility of being able to sack and appoint the trustee.

Clearly, this means the position of appointor is one of control and the appointment of this position needs to be made carefully.

There are a variety of types of trusts that can be set up including:

Discretionary trusts

These trusts are called **'discretionary' trusts** because the trustees have the 'discretion' to decide how much income, if any, is paid to each beneficiary and how often. These are commonly known as 'family' trusts and are used often in family businesses, and when no third parties are involved. This is because a person does not have a fixed interest in the asset held by the discretionary trust, and, as such, they are dependent upon the actions of the trustee in order to receive any benefit from it.

For example, if there were 10 beneficiaries and the trust made $100, it is totally up to the discretion of the trustee as to who gets what – he or she may decide to apportion the $100 equally into $10 benefits, or may decide to give the entire $100 to one beneficiary only.

It is this flexibility that makes discretionary trusts fantastic structures for evening out the income earnings of a property, business or even share portfolio. Income and capital gains can be distributed to the taxpayer earning the least in any particular year.

Sometimes circumstances change and incomes vary from year to year. Trusts give you the flexibility to change as your circumstances change.

Example:

Mum and Dad decide to buy an investment property. Mum works part-time and Dad is the major income earner. After much consideration they decide to buy the property in a discretionary trust. In the first few years the property makes a small tax loss.

This loss cannot be distributed as only profits can be distributed from a trust. The fact that the tax benefit of claiming the tax loss against Dad's income in the early years would be lost was known to Mum and Dad, however they bought the property for the long term and the long-term tax advantages on trust ownership outweighed the short-term tax-deduction.

As expected, in a few years the property was positively geared and the profits made on renting out the property

> **Cont'd:**
>
> could now be offset against the tax losses that were made in previous years, thus resulting in no tax being payable until all the losses were used up.
>
> Whilst Mum remained only working part time, any profits from the rental of the property (after using up any carried forward losses) would be distributed to Mum, with a little bit going to the children in unearned distributions up to their tax-free threshold.
>
> Similarly, if the property was sold, the capital gain could be distributed to Mum who would pay less tax than if the gain had to be distributed evenly, or even worse, solely to Dad. However, if Mum ever decided to return to full time work and her income matched that of Dad's, then the distribution of profits could be adjusted to reflect a more even distribution between Mum and Dad – or the use of a bucket company could be used to tax the profits.

Clearly, the utilisation of a trust structure through which to earn your income is not always an option, such as for salary and wage earners, or individuals who come under the personal services legislation of our Tax Act. However, I have seen too many clients wasting money by paying tax unnecessarily, when they are in businesses, and have investments where trusts could be used very effectively, and could have saved them thousands of dollars each year.

The following schedule shows how all the components of a discretionary trust fit together.

Diagram 1.1

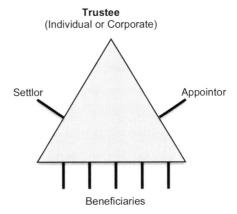

Unit trusts

Unit trusts work in a similar way to discretionary trusts, in that they both have a trustee, a settlor and in most cases, an appointor. However, instead of beneficiaries, a unit trust has unit holders. Unlike a discretionary trust beneficiary, a unit holder has an interest in the fixed, present legal entitlement to the assets of the trust. Consequently, on their own, unit trusts are not suitable vehicles for asset protection. However, when combined with other structures such as the discretionary trusts, they certainly have their uses.

Unit trusts are more suitable for businesses carried on by multiple parties. Each of the parties, by holding units in the unit trust, has a defined interest in the assets of that trust. In this respect, unit trusts are like companies, but instead of holding shares, the parties hold units in the unit trust.

Another benefit to a unit trust is that the units can be bought and sold. This is not possible with an interest in a discretionary trust.

A unit trust however does have some associated problems with respect to Capital Gains Tax, and in certain circumstances, depreciation.

Following, is a diagram of a basic unit trust structure:

Diagram 1.2

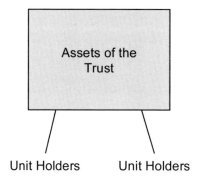

Hybrid Discretionary Trusts

A **hybrid discretionary trust** is simply made up of a combination of discretionary and unit trusts that best suits the needs of the company, family or individual. This type of trust is great for structuring businesses where you need to distinguish between who owns the asset or business, and who gets the income from the asset or business, because you may not necessarily want them to be the same.

This is how a hybrid trust would look:

Diagram 1.3

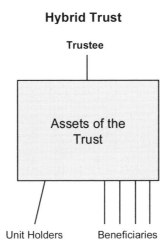

Putting a tax effective structure together

Okay, so we have looked at all the possible options of structures that are available to us. Now, how should we put it all together? Let's first consider the situation of someone in small business who wants to build a sizeable investment portfolio alongside their business activity.

Ideally, you would want to see both the business activity and the investment activity not only separated from each other, but for asset protection reasons, structured in such a way that income can be spread across the structures easily and losses from any negatively geared investment properties or business losses can be taken advantage of.

One solution would be to set up not only their business, but also their property, in a **company as a trustee for a trust**. This would not only give them the flexibility to distribute profits from the small business to the most tax efficient beneficiaries, it would also be ideal to take up the tax-deduction of a negatively geared investment as well as keeping assets separate for asset protection.

Ideally, their structure should look something like this:

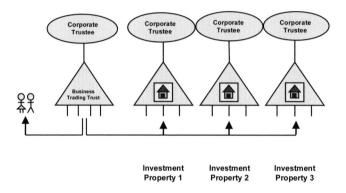

Flexible Income Distribution Model

The best way to fully understand the impact of this, is to look at an example. Let's consider the situation of Marge and Harry.

Example:

Marge and Harry are small business owners who run a hardware store. They have a profitable business and after paying themselves wages of 80,000 each, and contributing the maximum amount they can to superannuation, their hardware business still makes a sizeable profit of $100,000. Marge and Harry also have a couple of negatively geared investment properties that they bought some time ago for the purpose of getting a little bit of tax relief, as well as accumulating assets that would increase in value and create wealth for them for the longterm.

Now, had Marge and Harry set up their business directly into a company structure, in order to get a tax-deduction as a negative gearing benefit from the investment properties that they own, they would have also had to buy those investment properties either in the company's name directly or in their personal names.

Example:

At this stage you may be asking "why am I saying personal names?" Well you see Marg and Harry could take all the profit out of their company simply by paying themselves a higher wage. If they did that, the benefit of the extra tax-deductions gained from their negatively geared investment properties would then offset the salary that they are paying themselves from the company.

Had this been the case, that they did own the investment properties in their own name, of course Marge and Harry would be giving up any asset protection that could be gained by putting the properties into a separate structure. From a tax perspective however, Marge and Harry, as individuals, would be able to take advantage of the 50% Capital Gains Tax exemption and therefore reduce their tax when the properties were ultimately sold. This is not my favourite structure because of the asset protection implications or the lack thereof. Conversely, if they bought the investment properties directly in the company name, the negative gearing benefits could have been offset against the company profits directly.

The downside of this is that when those properties were sold, the company would not get any relief or the 50% Capital Gains Tax exemption, and therefore the company would pay double the amount of tax that they would have, had they bought the properties either in their company name or a trust structure. Again, this is not my favoured structure, as the asset protection is when you have a business and real property owned in the same structure. If there is ever a litigation originating from either the business or the properties, then the whole lot is up for grabs.

So how should Marge and Harry have set up their business and how does that structure interact with the structure that they should have set up for their investment properties?

Tax Secrets of a Real Estate Millionaire

If Marge and Harry had initially structured their business as a company as trustee for a discretionary trust, the trust could have been a hybrid (but that is probably overkill, since Marge and Harry are married and both are listed as primary beneficiaries of their own discretionary trust anyway), and any profits arising from the business could then be distributed to either Marge and Harry or any 'associated entity'.

These words, 'associated entity', are actually quite important, because if Marge and Harry's trust deed was set up correctly, they would have the flexibility to place additional profits in any structure; meaning another company, trusts, superannuation fund, etc., that they are associated with. So when it came to the investment properties, those investment properties could then have been purchased in separate discretionary trust structures. This would have given them not only asset protection away from themselves and their business, but it will also have allowed the profits from their business to be distributed to those trusts, which housed the negatively geared investment properties. Thus, their tax would be reduced on a year by year basis.

The example below shows how the additional excess profits, from their business, could be distributed directly up to their investment trusts to take up the negative gearing benefits:

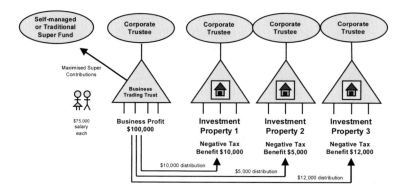

Example:

After Tax Distributions
Business trading profits yet to be distributed:

$ 100,000

Less
Distributed to Trust 1	$ 10,000
Distributed to Trust 2	$ 5,000
Distributed to Trust 3	$ 12,000

Balance $ 73,000

You will now note that Marge and Harry still have profits in their business to distribute somewhere. This is where the tax strategies start to become really interesting!

Because Marge and Harry are good little vegemites and they always go and see their accountant before the end of the financial year in about April or May, they have recognised that their profits for the year are extraordinarily high and they need to do something taxwise in order to avoid paying the top marginal tax rate on the extra profits.

Their accountant correctly advises them that it would be opportune to set up a 'bucket company' before the end of the financial year so that excess profits from their business could be distributed to the bucket company.

The bucket company would then pay tax on the excess profits at the company tax rate of 30 cents in the dollar.

For Marge and Harry this represents a tax saving of $7,300.

This is how Marge and Harry's tax structure would look now:

Tax Secrets of a Real Estate Millionaire

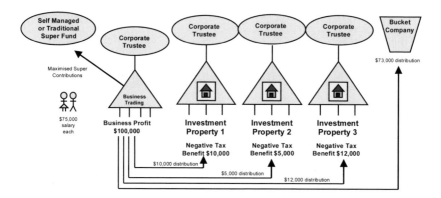

Note 1: *DIV7A changes means distributions to a corporate beneficiary must be either actually paid to the company and money transferred into the company bank account, or a commercial loan agreement must be signed and dealt with as any other commercial loan.*

Note 2: *For asset protection Marge and Harry should also have a discretionary 'piggybank' trust to own shares in the trustee company and any other non-leveraged shares, managed funds, gold, precious metal investments etc. See my book "Asset Protection Secrets of a Real Estate Millionaire"*

Example:

After Tax Bucket Company

	Income	$ 73,000
	Less Tax	$ 21,900
Tax Paid Available Money		$ 51,100

Tax Secrets of a Real Estate Millionaire

The next obvious question: How can Marge and Harry utilise the money that has already had 30% tax paid on it, sitting in their bucket company?

One solution would be to leave the money in the company. Let it accumulate over the years, add to it as excess profits are made and distributed to the bucket company where it pays tax, and in retirement, pay that money out to Marge and Harry when their marginal tax rates are much lower. Whilst this might be perfect for tax purposes, it is totally ineffective from an investment and wealth creation perspective.

A strategy that would benefit Marge and Harry more effectively would be to use the money sitting in the bucket company to lend out to new investment structures, such as the ones they already have and hold their existing investment properties in, as deposits for more investment properties. Of course, from a wealth creation perspective, this is not only going to create more wealth for them both in the short and long term, it would also mean that they would be able to retire earlier, compound their profits, and balance their portfolio with a selection of both positively and negatively geared investment property, or shares, or other investments. In time, Marge and Harry could utilise the business profits to build a significant real estate, share and cash investment portfolio which would look something like this.

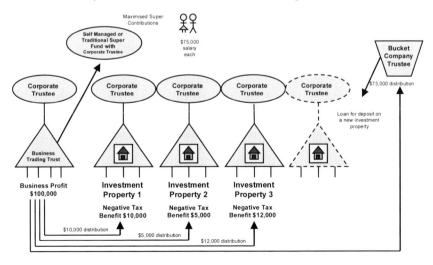

Note: *Marge and Harry would set up a loan from their bucket company to their newly formed trust for the deposit on their new investment property purchase. The balance of funds would come from an additional bank loan secured on the new investment property.*

Not everyone has the opportunity to earn their income through a business structure, and therefore not everyone has the opportunity to take advantage of the flexible income and tax structures above.

A great percentage of the population earn their income as a salary or wage earner. The main way that real estate tax losses can be offset against salary or wage income, is to own the investment property assets in the same name as the salary and wage earner. As you know, this is not something that I am particularly keen on, as the salary or wage earner is giving up all asset protection by owning everything in their own name. In Chapter 4, I will explain a complex tax structure which enables the salary and wage earner to purchase negatively geared investment properties through a trust structure (a hybrid trust structure) and still claim the negative gearing benefits that they would have been otherwise able to claim had they owned the property in their own names. Because through this method, the property is owned in a trust structure, the property is being asset protected as well as being tax efficient.

Basically, the type of trust you use and how you use it, are decisions that need to be made based on your individual situation. The most important thing to remember is that any use of a trust should be thoroughly investigated. Always carefully review the terms of the trust deed and seek professional advice whenever setting up a structure.

See our 'Benefits of Buying your Home through a Trust Structure' comparison table in Appendix H.

For more information about the uses of company structures for asset protection, see my book "Asset Protection Secrets of a Real Estate Millionaire"

> # Tax Tip:
>
> Even though the purpose of this book is to educate you on the taxation procedures and structures you need to reduce tax as a real estate investor, here is a tip for salary and wage earners who want to maximise their work tax-deductions.
>
> The Tax Office has fantastic tax-deduction publications on their website **www.ato.gov.au**. These publications detail all the allowable tax-deductions for just about every occupation you could possibly think of. I suggest you check it out for your occupation. You never know. You might be missing out on something!

Problems Using Old Trust Deeds

Changes to Tax/Trust Laws

There have been some changes to the Trust Law. First of all, there was a case called the Bamford Case.

The Bamfords sold a property back in 2002, I think it was. The distributions were made out of a Discretionary Trust in 2002 and 2003 to a number of beneficiaries. Because the sale was a capital sale, they were distributing capital down to the beneficiaries. A discretionary trust, is not a fixed trust, therefore you can distribute capital gains down and keep it as a capital gain, not treat it as income. Therefore you get the 50% exemption for Capital Gains Tax purposes.

In the Bamford's Case, the Tax Office decided to take Bamford to the court. It went all the way to the High Court. The decision came

Tax Secrets of a Real Estate Millionaire

down in March of 2010 - so from 2002 to March 2010 - it took that long to go through the legal proceedings. Can you imagine how much that would have cost? Enormous amounts of money.

Fortunately for the Bamfords, part of their distribution actually went to the Church of Scientology, and the Church of Scientology paid the court costs. The decision went the way of the Bamfords. Had it been somebody else, that didn't have the money to fight it, like the Church of Scientology, it would've been a situation where the use of trusts could have been in question. But they fought the good fight to the end and it went our way.

The result of this court case basically means your trust and your asset protection are as good as your trust deed's words. If you've got a well worded trust deed with good definitions of income and capital and distributions, then you're fine.

If you've got a badly worded trust deed then you probably will not be getting the 50% exemption on any Capital Gains Tax exemptions and it could be taxed at the highest marginal tax rate in the trust's name.

This is why I've been saying all the way along, when it comes to asset protection, don't go and just buy cheap stuff over the internet. There are cheapy little trust deeds that you can buy on the internet, and I can tell you now, some of them are not worth being used as toilet paper. There are others that might be okay, I don't know them all.

What the Bamford Case really highlights, is that you've got to have well worded trust deeds. You've got to be dealing with people who know the implications and have well worded trusts. This is why I give you access to so many people who can do that for you in the network. On top of that, it also means that anyone who has an existing trust deed now needs to take it and get it reviewed. The Bamford Case is a huge case when it comes to trust law.

There's some other changes about bucket companies. In particular

Division 7A which basically says that if you have distribution out of a trust going to a bucket company then two things have to happen. The money needs to physically go from the trust up to the bucket company into the bucket company's account and it then gets dealt with from there. You actually have to move the money. It is not just an accounting entry.

If money comes from a trust and gets distributed up to a corporate trustee, then you have to have a formal loan agreement in place. Interest must be paid at commercial rates, and it needs to be an arm's length transaction. There are changes as of December 2009, on the bucket company use, and these need to be taken into consideration also.

Chapter 4

Negative gearing exposed

This may sound harsh, but it astounds me how people who are normally sound-minded, logical and intelligent will make irrational, emotional decisions when it comes to investing in property! Over the years, I have seen hundreds and hundreds of my clients make investment decisions while they are on holidays. They take a vacation and think, "Hey, I'd like to have a holiday house here!" So they go off and buy an 'investment property', i.e. they buy the 'investment property' they would like to live in. Unfortunately, quite often that investment property is going to be hugely negatively geared, and it has *not* been selected for its potential growth. Quite likely, it has been selected because the kitchen looks great or the colour scheme was good, or they have been persuaded by the real estate agent, or it's around the corner from their friend's investment property.

These properties commonly have had $40,000 – $100,000 of the investor's equity, substituted equity, or actual savings invested in them.

Negative gearing has been part of the tax legislation for a very long time. It is the process of claiming a tax-deduction for the excess expenses relating to an income producing rental property against other taxable income.

The investor's goal is of course to have capital growth on their investment property, which outweighs any immediate negative cash flow effect.

Is buying negatively cash flowed property wrong?

Absolutely not. It may be a desirable thing in your circumstance. Maybe your portfolio needs maximum growth, rather than income or serviceability. Maybe you are already very strong on income and are able to withstand some degree of negative cash flow in order to maximise potential growth. You simply need to give due consideration to what is right for your portfolio.

For instance, you may have a reasonable job in which you feel quite comfortable. You may have some savings as a buffer, and in five years' time you may want to be able to cut back to part-time work, or even potentially take a year off. That being the case, you may like to consider:

- Focusing on a combination of both growth and income properties.

- Avoiding placing huge financial cash flow drains on your present income.

- Focusing on growth properties that are as close to neutrally geared as possible, but still have potential for significant growth over the 5 year time span.

- Being conscious of cash flow, and not overextending yourself with growth properties.

These are the types of decision-making processes that every successful investor needs to become familiar with. You need to be able to work out your next step according to the goals in your business plan: Should you purchase a growth property? If it is going to be a growth property, how much negativity in the cash flow department can your current circumstances withstand? On the other hand, should it be a positive cash flow property? In the circumstance where you require the income from a positive cash flow property, to balance off a negatively cash flowed property, make sure you do your numbers, and that you have sufficient cash flow being generated by that property to counter the negative cash flow on your growth properties.

- You would also need to bear in mind that in focusing only on 'cash cows', you will eventually run out of equity to continue investing. It's the *growth* properties that create the equity, but that's a topic for another time.

- These are all financing considerations and limitations which seem to be swept under the carpet when someone's buying an investment property. Interestingly, the successful purchasing of property comes down to being worldly or street smart, rather than who has the best (academic) education or the finance degree. Being able to assess the profitability of your property, business and/or investment is really very simple. The calculations are very straightforward and fundamentally come down to common sense:

- How much income does my property investment generate?

- How much do I have to spend on it?

- Is it positively cash flowed or not?

- Can I service it, if it is negatively cash flowed?

- What do I believe my chances are of that property going up in value?

- If I purchase this property, what do I think is going to happen?

Do you know what this is all essentially about? It's about:

- **you** being a business manager

- **you** gaining sufficient knowledge and education through due diligence, studying, extra courses and seminars to increase your knowledge, so that you can determine the best thing for you to do next

- **you** understanding your budget

- **you** understanding the due diligence processes

- **you** understanding what your goals and aspirations are, and what strategies you can employ to achieve them.

That's right it's all about **you**! It's about you and your objectives, ultimately. *And,* it's a matter of selecting the best strategy that suits your ultimate objectives, along with your personality, to achieve your goals.

Tax Secrets of a Real Estate Millionaire

More than likely, your ideal portfolio and strategy for the future is going to incorporate a balance of both growth and income properties – manufactured or direct. Your strategy is not going to be solely one or the other. The fact is though, that you are never going to know what that ideal portfolio or strategy is, unless you start thinking about your future investments as a business.

Be worldly!
Be streetwise!
Have common sense!

Take the emotion out of investing

When I'm talking about taking the emotion out of investing, I'm realistic enough to know that this won't apply to your principal place of residence (PPR). That is usually a lifestyle decision and maybe even a potential investment decision.

Factors such as children's schooling and proximity to amenities, where you like to live, even down to the colour of the kitchen, etc., tend to be more acceptable as decision-making factors when purchasing your PPR.

> "Do not make an investment decision based solely on tax - it should be a good investment first - tax efficient second"

What I am talking about is taking the emotion out when you are purchasing an investment property - that's what it is: *an investment*. Therefore, the decision-making process should be more about the numbers, the analysis, the statistics behind *why* you are making that decision, and what you are endeavouring to achieve for your portfolio - and less about your emotions.

I'll put it this way - how many people would actually buy a business that lost money every year? Truly, that's what happens to thousands and thousands of property investors. They buy properties that don't cash flow. Some of them buy properties that cost them money every single week!

Now obviously they justify this decision by rationalising, "Oh, but property goes up in value." Yes, that's true, but when I have quizzed my clients on the decision-making process as to what due diligence has led to the selection of one particular property over another, or on what rationale they have calculated the potential growth of one property over another, they are left speechless.

I know clients who have five or six negatively geared properties, which means they have got to service the negative cash flow from their other income – whether it be a wage or a salary or passive income that they may have been able to achieve on other property. This type of investing behaviour only ties them to a job and keeps them in the rat race for life. If you want to have choices, have lifestyle, have early retirement (whatever that means), and have the life you want, you have to be a much more savvy investor than just buying one negatively geared investment property after another.

In most cases, the investment decision-making process has been an emotional one, not a business one. Are you getting the picture I am painting for you yet?

What do you think that same holidaying couple would do if they were presented with a business purchase which required a capital or equity investment from them of between $40,000 - $100,000? Would they do it because they liked the colour of the prospectus or the vendor's hair colour or because their friend said so? With $40,000 - $100,000 at stake, we know that couple would want to be completely informed about the investment.

In fact, far more due diligence would be done, and their rationale for assessing that business would be completely different, wouldn't it? Of course it would! They would want to know the potential return of the investment – not just now, but into the future. They would want to know the latest growth statistics of that particular market. They would want to know the likelihood of the investment not being able to return an income at any point in time, and whether or not they could service the debt. Now, compare this to purchasing 'investment property' because the kitchen looks good or your friend said so!

Can you see my point?

Create a plan

What any astute investor needs to do is put together a plan - a business plan for their personal financial future. Your financial future is a business, so treat it with the same respect you would if you were buying a business.

Without having a plan, you are inadvertently planning to fail. You need to treat the purchasing of property as a business because any individual investment purchase *is* a business.

Think about it - a business has income, it has expenses, it has growth, hopefully, and you have either a profit or a loss at the end of the day. A property is no different. It too, has income and expenses. It too, has the potential to go up in value.

In both, you invest considerable amounts of time, money or equity, so why wouldn't you do all the necessary due diligence and analysis regarding the purchase of property, as you would if you were buying a business? Get very clear that you are in the *business* of purchasing investment property, and as such, you are entitled to the tax-deductions awarded to businesses.

When you run a business, all your expenses related to that business are tax-deductible against the income of the business. This is the same when you run an investment property business. All your expenses or interest on the mortgage, council rates, insurance, body corporate, management fees etc., are all deductibles offset against the income the property earns.

Tax Secrets of a Real Estate Millionaire

The extra benefit and tax boost that you get when you are in the business of investment properties, is a tax-deduction for not spending any money!

No, I'm not going crazy.

The taxation legislation since 1985 has allowed a tax-deduction for the diminishing value of your asset; being the building and specifically the fixtures and fittings of that building.

It's called 'depreciation'. It's a tax-deduction based on a Tax Office approved formula which you get regardless of the fact that you are not actually spending money on your investment property.

The depreciation benefit is a short-term benefit, as any tax benefits you gain whilst you own the property are added back into the calculation for calculating Capital Gains Tax on the property when you sell it.

> "depreciation is the deduction you get without spending any money"

However, even though this is the case, maximising your depreciation tax-deductions while they are available means that tax is ultimately deferred to when you sell the property. This could be way into the future, and even when the property is eventually sold, the tax liability would be halved due to the 50% Capital Gains Tax exemption available on sale, provided the property has been owned for more than 12 months and in a tax efficient structure or entity.

It's a crazy concept - getting something from the Tax Office for nothing. Well, almost nothing. They do give you a little sting and have the final say when you sell the property.

Some people are vehement supporters of negative gearing and others are vehemently against negative gearing. I am more on the vehemently against – but still recognise in some circumstances, negative gearing is necessary to achieve good growth on desirable properties. I believe negative gearing is something that can be very, very useful in certain circumstances, whereas in other circum-stances, particularly when overused, it can leave the investor cash-strapped and on the verge of going bankrupt.

I believe the ideal use of negative gearing is when a property fits certain criteria. That criteria is when the property is actually cash flow positive yet cash negative for tax purposes. If your investing goal is income replacement, forget the negative gearing and concentrate on cash flow positive with manufactured growth, to allow for continuity of investment.

The style of property that fits the cash flow positive but tax negative criteria is usually a property that is either new or near new or has had major renovations carried out on the property recently, and these capital improvements can be quantified with a quantity surveyor report. This way, the free tax-deductions for depreciation can be maximised, and therefore the negative gearing tax benefits are high, but the cash flow can still be positive in real terms. Let me show you an example of how this works.

> "negative gearing is over used and over sold – it is tax derived poverty"

Example:

Let's assume we have an investor with a salary of $45,000, who is considering buying an investment property worth $225,000.

Let's also assume that he will be paying an interest rate of 7% and that by using equity available in his home, he is able to borrow and claim a full tax-deduction for 100% of the purchase price plus costs.

Example:

Purchase Price	$	225,000
Legal Fees	$	650
Stamp Duty (estimate)	$	6,400
Loan App. Fees	$	2,000
	$	234,050

Interest rates 7%
Rental Income

$ 20,000

Less

Interest Payment	$	16,380
Rates	$	1,200
Body Corporate Fees	$	765
Management Fees	$	1,700
Letting Fees	$	385
Insurance	$	350
Maintenance	$	200
	$	20,980

Net Annual Cash Shortfall $ 980
or $18.85 per week

So on the face of it – this property is negatively geared - although only slightly.

However, the above calculation does not take into account any depreciation which may be able to be claimed on this property, nor does it take into account the tax-deduction which can be claimed over five years for the borrowing expenses.

Let's have a look at how these additional losses are calculated.

Example:

Depreciation:

Deprec. on fixtures and fitting $20,000 @ 20%	$ 4,000
Deprec. on building $104,000 @ 2.5%	$ 2,600
Deprec. on fixtures and fittings $2,500 @ 100%	$ 2,500
Amortisation of borrowing costs	$ 9,100
Borrowing costs amortised over 5 years	$ 400
Total depreciation losses	**$ 9,500**

Paper Losses

You will notice that some fixtures and fittings have been claimed at a depreciation rate of 20% whereas a small amount of fixtures and fittings have been claimed at 100% depreciation. This is because some items can be expensed fully in the first year of purchase. Obviously, this deduction would not be available to the investor in the second or subsequent tax years.

See Appendix D for full list of rental property depreciation schedules.

When you take the actual cash flow shortfall and the paper losses into account on the next page, you will see how our investor's tax would be affected. On first appearances, this property appears to be cash flow negative. However, when the tax effect of the paper losses is taken into account, the property is actually positively cash flowed by $73.92 a week.

Example:

Gross salary	$ 90,000
Less Deductions	
- cash shortfall	$ 980
- paper losses	$ 9,500
Adjusted Taxable Income	$ 79,520

This means that instead of paying tax on a salary of $90,000, our investor will pay tax on $79,520. Here is what the net tax saving will be to our investor for owning this property in the first year.

Tax payable on $90,000	$ 21,247
Tax payable on $79,520	$ 17,391
Tax saving	$ 3,856
	or $74.15/wk

Figures exclude medicare levy

Ideally, if investors have a good, strong income from salary, business or investments, choosing this style of investment property provides them with the best of both worlds. That is, a tax-deduction to help reduce tax payable on their other income, and a positive cash flow which can be used to support living, lifestyle or further investment.

This really is, having your cake and eating it too!

Chapter 5

Negative gearing nuances

I am often asked the question, "Why can't I utilise the benefits of negative gearing and not hold the asset in my own name for asset protection purposes?" Well, there have been many structures set up using hybrid trusts to do exactly that. The difficulty is the Tax Office has constantly narrowed the use of such a trust with legal cases like *FC of T v. Janmor Nominees Pty Ltd* 87 ATC 4813; (1987) 19 ATR 254 and a more recent case *Fletcher & Ors v. FC of T 91 ATC 4950* as well as other private rulings, to the point where the use of a hybrid trust for negative gearing has become dubious at best, and highly risky at worst.

This is how it works.

Tax Secrets of a Real Estate Millionaire

Negative gearing through a hybrid trust

A taxpayer with a high salary and equity in his/her own home can use the equity to get a loan for the deposit on an investment property. Instead of using the equity as a deposit directly on the new investment property, the taxpayer can subscribe to income units in a hybrid trust. The unit trust in turn uses the funds as a deposit on the desired investment property, and the hybrid trust then borrows the additional monies required to purchase the property from a bank. This way, the taxpayer can benefit from expenses as a unit holder in the hybrid trust, and claim any negative gearing against his/her taxable income.

Example:

David buys a property through a hybrid trust for $300,000. He borrows $60,000 against the equity in his home from a bank, and with the $60,000 buys 60,000 units at $1.00 each from the hybrid trust. The remaining $240,000 needed to buy the property is borrowed from the bank through the hybrid trust, using the $60,000 as the deposit. Let's assume the interest rate is 8%, and that the trust rents the house out for $300 p/w and has income and expenditure for the year as follows:

Rental Income	$ 15,600
Less	
Management Fees	$ 1,170
Rates	$ 1,100
Insurance	$ 500
Depreciation	$ 2,500
Interest	$ 19,200
Total Expenses	$ 24,470
Loss	$ 8,870

The loss from the hybrid trust cannot be distributed to unit holders, so the loss has no benefit to David's immediate tax situation. It can however, be accumulated and offset against future income earned by the hybrid trust. However, because David borrowed the $60,000 that he purchased the units with, any interest and bank fees can be negatively geared and claimed against his taxable income.

Example:

	Salary	$ 78,000
	Tax Payable	$ 16,897

With 60,000 units purchased in a hybrid trust:

Interest on $60,000 Loan @ 8%	$ 4,800
Salary after Deductions	$ 73,200
Tax Payable	$ 15,337
Tax Savings	$ 1,560

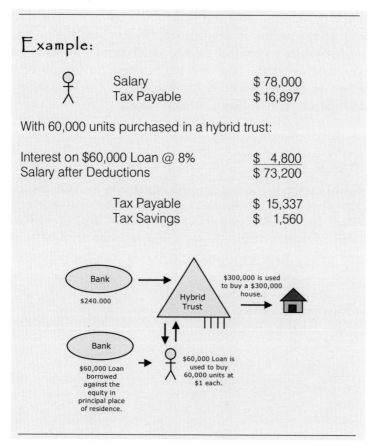

*Figures exclude medicare levy

Now let's step up the game here a little.

If David had borrowed the entire $300,000 and bought 300,000 units in the hybrid trust, the proceeds of which would then be used to purchase that same house, and he was able to structure a lending facility with his bank or financial institution such that the bank accepted the new house being purchased in the trust, as partial security for the loan, the result would have been quite different. A greater tax-deduction from his taxable income would have been able to be claimed even though the hybrid trust would have made a taxable profit which would need to be distributed.

This is how the figures would work:

Example:

	Salary	$ 78,000
	Trust Income	$ 10,330
	Total Income	$ 88,330
	Tax Payable	$ 20,629

With 300,000 units purchased in a hybrid trust:

Interest on $300,000 Loan @ 8%	$ 24,000
Salary after Deductions	$ 64,330
Tax Payable	$ 12,454
Tax Savings	$ 8,175

Hybrid Trust

$300,000 is used to buy $300,000 house.

Bank — $300,000 Loan borrowed against the equity in principal place of residence.

$300,000 Loan is used to buy 300,000 units at $1 each.

*Figures exclude medicare levy

Tax Secrets of a Real Estate Millionaire

This is how the Hybrid Trust income with the previous arrangement would look:

Example:

Rental Income	$ 15,600
Management Fees	$ 1,170
Rates	$ 1,100
Insurance	$ 500
Depreciation	$ 2,500
Total Expenses	$ 5,270
Profit	$ 10,330

The after-expenses income of the trust is distributed to David as a return on his income units. Whilst the flexibility of a hybrid trust normally does allow distributions to be made to other lower income earners, I believe all the income should be distributed to the owner of the hybrid trust units, as this would be the situation if the property was owned directly in the taxpayer's name.

Also, whilst the income of the hybrid trust could have remained undistributed in the trust, and the trustee could have paid tax on behalf of the trust, this would have been a ridiculous decision, as the trust would have paid tax at up to 66%, which is a much higher tax rate than David, our taxpayer.

To further this scenario, after a number of years, David might decide that he would like to sell his 300,000 units back to the trust so that he can either pay back the balance of the loan or use the money to buy something else.

Example:

David sells his 300,000 units in the hybrid trust back to the trust on money that the trust has borrowed from the bank.

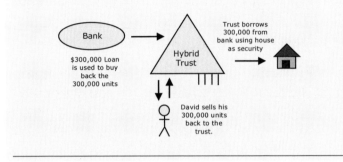

The bonus with this arrangement is that David gets his $300,000 back tax-free, because he is not making a profit on the units – the trust buys them back at the same price that he bought them for. Additionally, the trust can now claim the interest being paid on the loan for the purchase of the units as a tax-deduction all over again!

At some stage, as trustee for the hybrid trust or rather, as director of the corporate trustee, David might decide to sell the property. As it was bought in a growth area and over the years has been improved, it has made a capital gain, which of course means that the trust will have capital gains to distribute. At this point, rather than distribute the gain to himself and have to pay the high marginal tax rate on the capital gain, it would be more advantageous to distribute the money to low income beneficiaries such as his wife (who currently has no income), or to his children, so as to take advantage of a lower tax rate, and thus reducing the Capital Gains Tax payable.

Now all that sounds really good doesn't it?

Tax Secrets of a Real Estate Millionaire

A big fat warning!

Well, here is a **HUGE WARNING!** The future of such strategies is unclear, and before entering into this type of arrangement, you should seek the advice of your accountant and even apply for a private ruling on your particular set of circumstances. A private ruling is binding, so if the Tax Office says it is OK in your circumstances then go ahead, but if not, well, you have your answer.

The cost of a private ruling is really only the cost of time spent by your accountant preparing the appropriate wording of the paper, and stating the correct legal argument so that the result can be relied on when given from the Tax Office.

Other areas of concern

There is also another school of thought that says, if David wants to claim the negative gearing tax benefits from the purchase of the property in a trust – he should not only subscribe to income units but should also have some growth units attached to his initial subscription for units. This would mean that the growth/capital gain, when either his units are redeemed and/or the property is sold, would be distributed to him.

I believe that money to be made from the investment in real estate and the pro-active strategies to accumulate wealth and replace income should be the driving force behind investment decisions – not tax. Tax should be legally minimised, of course, but the fundamental rationale should be to make money.

Depending on what type of property you buy, and what the yield is on the property, the negative gearing benefits usually only last for about five years – after which the property is probably neutral or cash flow positive anyway. At this time, positive cash flow will be taxed at the taxpayer's marginal tax rate which is probably high. At least if the property is in a trust you have the flexibility to place the income anywhere the trustee sees fit.

I certainly would not be setting up a hybrid trust for negative gearing purposes, nor would I like to be the accountant that is setting one up for a client. I believe the ATO treatment of them is too shakey. I wouldn't want to be another Bamford and end up in the high court.

Chapter 6

The flipside.., positive gearing

On the flipside of negative gearing, you have positive gearing. Obviously, when a property is positively geared, what we are talking about is having a property that produces more income than it costs you. When a property produces more income than it costs you, it means that more rent comes in than all of the expenses added together (the rates, the insurance, the management fees, all of the repairs and any other expenses to do with the property). When you have taken off all of these expenses you still have money left.

Now, when you have got money left, from a tax perspective that means of course, you have to pay tax. When you pay tax on a positively geared property it is going to be taxed at your normal marginal tax rates.

Tax Secrets of a Real Estate Millionaire

Any income that you earn in your own name from any rental properties that you have, will be added onto your other salary. It will be added to any other income that you might have from other businesses or jobs or whatever else you earn in your own name. This means that the extra amount that you are earning from a positively cash flowed property would be taxed at your marginal tax rate.

In Australia, we use a system where tax is calculated on what is referred to as a 'marginal scale' with different 'tax brackets' and different rates of tax to pay depending on what your level of taxable income is. The first of these brackets is everyone's favourite, because, at the moment the law says the first $18,200 is income is tax-free. Then we have the next 'bracket' as we call it, from $18,201 to $37,000. This means that any income that is earned over $18,200 but less than $37,000, you will pay 19 cents in the dollar - 19% tax. Income of $37,001 and over will be taxed at 32.5 cents in the dollar and it goes up accordingly.

See Appendix G for tax bracket tables.

For instance, if you earn $40,000 year, your first $18,200 will be tax-free. For the next amount that you earn to between $18,201 and $37,000, you will pay 19 cents in the dollar, and any money that you earn above that i.e. $3,000, you pay 32.5 cents in the dollar. *That* is what a 'marginal tax rate' actually means.

So when I say any rental income that you have will be taxed at your 'marginal tax rate' and you're on say, in this example, $40,000 a year, then your tax rate on your marginal tax rate is 32.5%. This means that if you have a positively cash flowed property that produces you $5,000 a year positive cash flow from the extra rental that you receive over and above all of the expenses on the property, then you will pay 32.5 cents in the dollar or 32.5% on that extra $5,000 ($5000 x 0.325 = $1,625 tax).

That's how it works.

Tax Secrets of a Real Estate Millionaire

Cash Flow Analysis

Income:
Estimated Annual Gross Rental Income _____
Other Income _____
    Total Gross Income _____
    Less Vacancy Allowance _____
    Effective Gross Income _____

Expenses:
Body Corporate Fees _____
Rates _____
Insurance _____
Water / Sewer _____
Garbage _____
Electricity _____
Licenses _____
Advertising / Letting Fees _____
Supplies _____
Maintenance _____
Lawn _____
Pest Control _____
Management (off site) _____
Management (on site) _____
Accounting / Legal _____
Miscellaneous _____
Gas _____
Telephone _____
Pools _____
Elevator _____
Budget for Replacements _____
    Total Expenses _____
    Net Operating Income _____

Debt Service:
1st Mortgage _____
2nd Mortgage _____
Total Debt Service _____

Cash Flow: _____

Tax Secrets of a Real Estate Millionaire

Positive? Negative? How will I know?

Now you might ask; how on earth am I going to know whether my property is positively geared or negatively geared or know what can happen through the year? From time to time your property may have had a few more expenses, or it may have had a couple of weeks where it was vacant, which might change whether or not the property can produce the full year of income. Maybe it had to have a fence replaced, or other repairs, and you're not really sure whether this year the property will be positively or negatively geared.

What I absolutely recommend...

Is to go and see your accountant around about that April/May timeframe so you can review everything that you have done over the year. Whether it is from your work, small businesses or real estate investing, by going in before the end of the financial year you have then got the opportunity to make the necessary adjustments to your tax, to make it as advantageous as you possibly can make it for the year.

For instance, let's say that you have a really big year at work and you've had commissions coming in as well as a couple of bonuses or other things that might boost your income, so your Income Tax for the year is extraordinarily higher than it normally is. Let's say also that your income is such that those extra few bonuses of income push you up into the next tax bracket. Then of course by doing that, instead of being on a possible 32.5 cents in the dollar you might now be on 37 or 45 cents in the dollar, marginal tax rate. This means you will be paying a lot more tax on that extra little bit of positive cash flow rent that you are collecting.

If you know that and you are reviewing things around that April/May period, at that point in time you can really decide and estimate what your taxable income is likely to be for that year. If after your estimation you find that you have actually pushed your income into the next tax bracket, you then have the option of bringing forward any expenses that you were going to spend on rental properties, into this financial year, as opposed to it being expensed in next financial year as it may otherwise have been.

A perfect example of this was a doctor client of mine. I remember when I was sitting in my accountancy practice and he came to see me. I had trained him very, very well so he came to see me April/May every year to have what I call a pre-year end review.

He'd had a bumper year and he'd earned alot more than he had in previous years and he was whinging about just how much tax he was going to have to pay. He had this defeatist attitude and he sat there and said, "Well, there's nothing more we can do, no matter how I look at my figures, I have had this big year and I am going to have to pay all this tax."

He was feeling terribly sorry for himself, but after talking to him for a considerable amount of time and extracting information from him (which was like pulling teeth), I started to ask him 'third level' questions. With these questions he started telling me what he had done during the year, and where he had been, and why his income was higher than normal.

I discovered the things that had led up to this bumper year. He actually owned hospitals and had been to a number of medical conventions. He had been on a little bit of a holiday (he was of English background) and he went back to England to see family. While he was there, he went to some conventions and met up with a few old work colleagues, allowing him to do a couple of deals resulting in the income for the hospital being a lot higher than it would have normally been.

I asked him if all of these expenses were included in his books and he said that he hadn't included them as he thought it was just a holiday. So, by going through and reorganising his expenses, taking in the costs of him going over there (not his wife and kids, just him) and attending these conventions and all of the other associated peripheral expenses that led to that actual trip, we were able to calculate the trip into his expenses and thus reduce his tax in such a way that we saved him around about $80,000 - $90,000 in tax. *That,* is how much of a difference it can actually make.

Now the other thing I did with this particular doctor was to ask him how the hospital was going and what he anticipated it was going to be like next year. He thought that next year's profits were not likely to be as large as he has to do all of these things such as paint, repairs and a number of other improvements. Again he was defeatist and stated that he wouldn't have any money to do it all, because this year he was going to have to pay it all on taxes.

Hang on a minute! Because we were still in April/May we were able to look and see if we could make some of that expenditure in the current financial year rather than next financial year, which meant that the tax bill for this financial year would be lowered.

So again, we went back to the drawing board and thought about all of things that needed to be done on the hospital. These were all the things that he was going to spend money on anyway, but instead of doing them over the next 6 to 12 months, we brought forward that expenditure and put it in the year where we had an extraordinarily high income, meaning for that year we had basically negated out all of that extra income. At the end of the day, when we finished playing around with all his taxes, we ended up paying around $200,000 less than he would have had to otherwise. So I figured it was a pretty fair day's work!

There needs to be a 'connection' or 'nexus'!

It is important to remember that the deductibility of expenses has to have a connection to the income that you are currently earning. It can't be a connection to an income that you might earn in the future by changing careers or doing something else.

It's called having a 'nexus' (from the Latin meaning 'to bind' or 'join'), or a connection, to the income. The expenses must have a nexus or a connection to the income that you are actually earning.

For instance, if you are a plumber and you are studying first aid so that you can be a part-time ambulance driver, you can't claim that as a tax-deduction because it has nothing to do with your current stream of income, which is earning income as a plumber.

If this same plumber set up a business where he was contracting himself out as a lifeguard, an ambulance officer, a safety officer for a company or something similar and he is set up as a separate business, and part of setting up this business is the expense to get his tickets, training and everything else in relation to first aid, then that would be an expense against that business.

In a separate structure, that loss could now be carried forward to be offset against any future income that he might have relating to that business, but it could not be offset against his plumbing income. It would just get carried forward to be offset against future income relating to that separate business and can continue to be carried forward to future years providing it is within reason.

Think like a business. Really think about all the things that you can start to claim tax-deductions for, and if they possibly relate to the income that you are earning.

Positive cash flow properties

I guess when you start talking about positive cash flow properties, the biggest question I always get asked is, "Should I be buying a positive cash flow property or a negative cash flow property?" The answer to this question is not so much a tax question, but more a question of what suits your investing portfolio and your short and medium term goals.

Most people, when making this decision, get hung up on the tax issues of positively cash flowed properties and negatively cash flowed properties, rather than focusing on the real issue of what's right from an investment perspective, and which style of property is going to give them the best investment result. Once this decision is made, that's when you should start to focus on tax and look at the best and most tax efficient way of actually buying the asset.

Let me work through an example:

Example:

Year 1

$100,000 Salary

Investment 1 + cash flow $ 5,000

Investment 2 + cash flow $ 4,500

Year 2

Investment 3 + cash flow $12,000

Investment 4 + cash flow $ 6,000

Year 3

Investment 5 + cash flow $ 6,000

Investment 6 + cash flow $10,000

Year 4

Investment 7 + cash flow $ 5,000

Investment 8 + cash flow $ 8,000

Investment 9 + cash flow $ 5,000

Total: 9 Investments + cash flow $61,500

Owned as an individual, tax on additional income is as follows:

Year 1	$ 3,515
Year 2	$ 10,175
Year 3	$ 16,095
Year 4	$ 22,755

*excludes Medicare Levy

Tax Secrets of a Real Estate Millionaire

Let's assume our investor has a salary and wage income of $100,000. Let's assume that our investor's goal is to replace his income over the next four to five years. Let's also assume that he is quite happy in his salary or wage job at the moment, but in four to five years he would like to take a year off and maybe even go back to study to change careers.

Now, the question most people ask is, "Should our investor focus on growth assets, which were probably going to be negatively geared, or positive cash flow assets, which will produce him a passive income, and over time, he could accumulate these types of positive cash flow properties so that in four to five years, he could have totally replaced his income?"

This is a tricky one, because both strategies will work if used properly. From a tax perspective, any excess income from his positive cash flow properties that are bought whilst he is still working in his job, will be taxed at his marginal tax rate, unless of course he chooses to buy these properties in a trust structure so that any positive cash flow could then be distributed to either a lower income spouse or a bucket company as described in Chapter 3.

However, if our investor was a little bit smarter and was conscious of asset protection, he would have bought these properties, not as an individual, but in a trust structure, so that any distribution could be placed wherever the income would be taxed at the lowest marginal tax rate.

If we assume our investor is a single person or doesn't have his spouse on a lower income rate, then he would utilise a bucket company to pay the tax on the additional money.

This would mean all his additional income would be taxed at the company tax rate of 30%. His Income Tax payable on the additional income would now look something like this:

> **Example:**
> If property is owned in a trust structure and distributed to a bucket company, tax on additional income would be as follows:
>
> | | |
> |---|---|
> | Year 1 | $ 2,850 |
> | Year 2 | $ 8,250 |
> | Year 3 | $13,050 |
> | Year 4 | $18,450 |
>
> Total tax saving through a trust structure as opposed to individual ownership is $4,305

Alternatively, our investor could focus on negatively geared growth investments from which he could service the cash flow shortage from his salary or wage, and hope that the growth in the properties over the four to five years is sufficient so that in this time, some of the properties could be sold, and the profits used to reduce debt on the remaining properties.

This is a common debt reduction strategy used by high income earners in order to have a tax benefit now, with the ability to hold good core assets with low debt levels in the future.

Our investor though, would have to be careful as to when these properties were actually sold so that they weren't being sold in a year when his taxable income was still high.

This would defeat the purpose of his previous tax savings as any capital gain would be taxed at the higher marginal tax rate.

Example:

  $100,000 Salary

Year 1

Investment 1 negative cash flow $ 10,000

Investment 2 negative cash flow $ 5,000

Year 2

Investment 3 negative cash flow $ 5,000

Investment 4 negative cash flow $ 5,000

Our investor is now feeling the squeeze – cash flow is tight and he is wondering whether this investment game is worth it.

Year 3 & 4
Can't afford to buy another negatively geared property – no purchases are made.

Let's assume our investor bought properties valued at an average of $250,000 in the first year and $275,000 in the second year.

Let's also assume that our investor bought well and selected areas which grew at 10%, and that when he purchased the properties he borrowed 100% of the purchase price each time.

At the end of the four years his investment portfolio would look something like this:

Example:

	Purchase Price	Value with Gwth	Loan
Year 1			
	$250,000 +10% Gwth	$275,000	$250,000
	$250,000 +10% Gwth	$275,000	$250,000
Year 2			
	$275,000 +10% Gwth	$302,500 (Existing)	$250,000
	$275,000 +10% Gwth	$302,500 (Existing)	$250,000
	$275,000 +10% Gwth	$302,500 (New)	$275,000
	$275,000 +10% Gwth	$302,500 (New)	$275,000
Year 3 – no new purchases			
	$302,500 + 10% Gwth	$332,750	$250,000
	$302,500 + 10% Gwth	$332,750	$250,000
	$302,500 + 10% Gwth	$332,750	$275,000
	$302,500 + 10% Gwth	$332,750	$275,000
Year 4 – no new purchases			
	$332,500 + 10% Gwth	$366,025	$250,000
	$332,500 + 10% Gwth	$366,025	$250,000
	$332,500 + 10% Gwth	$366,025	$275,000
	$332,500 + 10% Gwth	$366,025	$275,000

Total Property Value $ 1,464,100-
Total Loan Value $ 1,050,000
Net Equity $ 414,100

Tax Secrets of a Real Estate Millionaire

I know which one I would prefer – I'd take the passive income of $60,000 for life (indexed) any day over a $400,000 lump sum. The negative gearing road ties you to your job – whereas the passive income road gives you freedom to go and do whatever you want for the rest of your life, including continuing to invest.

Chapter 7

Maximise your tax strategy

Whilst the tax law is like a partnership agreement with the Tax Office, it is your responsibility to maximise your tax benefits so that your share of the profits is as large as possible. To do this, you need to know how the tax laws work and how they affect you in your particular industry - so let's get into the 'nitty gritty'.

Use tax-deductions to generate real estate cash flow

When you buy an investment property, you are entitled to deduct expenses that relate to that specific rental property and therefore not pay tax on that amount of income that the property produces. However, ownership of property also gives you tax benefits or tax-deductions for the depreciating value of the building, and in most cases the fixtures and fittings in the building.

Effectively, this is a tax-deduction or tax benefit for **FREE**. What this means is that on some property, large amounts of income produced by the property can be tax-free.

Tax Department found inefficient

What types of real estate maximise tax-free income?

Real estate with the registered quantity surveyor's report

A quantity surveyor is a person who estimates the amount and cost of various materials, labour and items in a property, construction or project, and reports this in writing through a Quantity Surveyor's Report. To submit a Property Tax Allowances claim to the Tax Office, an investor should request a property tax allowances schedule from a professionally qualified person.

Quantity surveyors are professionally qualified persons under Tax Ruling 97/25, and their schedule will substantiate an investor's depreciation claim upon lodgement of their tax return with the Tax Office.

Tax Secrets of a Real Estate Millionaire

It pays to shop around. Over the years I have seen many Quantity Surveyor's Reports whilst lodging tax returns, and some are very comprehensive and detailed with pages and pages of deductible depreciation on itemised fittings and structures which the owner is entitled to claim.

On the other hand, some are very lightweight, and the extra tax-deductions and subsequent tax saved barely make it worth paying a quantity surveyor to prepare the report. Ask to see sample copies of the Quantity Surveyor's Report, and make sure paying their fee will be worthwhile and the extra tax-deductions will justify the cost.

Overall, spending money on a Quantity Surveyor's Report should make you money, not cost you money. Another thing to keep an eye out for, is that the Quantity Surveyor's Report provides you with the options to claim your depreciation either on a 'prime cost method' or 'diminishing value method'. I will explain the difference a bit later.

> " the cost of employing a Quantity Surveyor is tax-deductible"

Long gone are the days when you or your accountant could make up a list of deductible items in your newly purchased rental property. A tax-deduction will not be allowed for depreciation on fixtures and fittings or building writeoffs, unless you have a report from a suitable qualified quantity surveyor. The Tax Office will not argue with a bona fide Quantity Surveyor's Report as the Tax Office have had discussion and agreements with the Australian Institute of Quantity Surveyors to ensure that members of this professional body are following all relevant standards. The cost of having a Quantity Surveyor's Report prepared is of course tax-deductible.

Newly constructed real estate

New or near new properties have more available depreciation than older properties where the previous owners have taken advantage of most of the available tax-deductions already.

Most of the available tax-deductions are used up in the first five years of owning the property. This is because you get the greatest tax-deduction for fixtures and fittings - usually up to around the 20% mark in the first five years.

> "it is advisable to ask the seller of a property if they ever had a Quantity Surveyor's report prepared on the property and if so, ask for a copy of the report"

These fixtures and fittings would include items such as light fittings, furniture, pool pumps, carpets, curtains, blinds etc.

Of course, depreciation on the cost of construction or the capital works will last much longer than five years, and in most newly constructed properties, the capital works deduction will be written off over forty years. There have been periods of time in the past when the tax law has changed, and for buildings constructed during those timeframes, a capital works deduction was actually allowed over a twenty-five year timeframe. A more comprehensive list of these dates and corresponding capital works depreciation rates can be viewed in Appendix E.

It is for this reason that new home construction companies really push the benefits of negative gearing and offsetting high levels of depreciation in the first five years of ownership to investors with moderate to high taxable incomes, who believe it is their God-given right not to pay tax. Claiming a tax-deduction for depreciation on investment properties is a way of achieving this, as explained in more detail in Chapter 4.

Tax Secrets of a Real Estate Millionaire

Many sellers of house and land packages and new construction housing supply a Quantity Surveyor's Report with the sale of the property. If the seller of a property you are intending to purchase hasn't provided you with a Quantity Surveyor's Report prior to purchase, it is a good idea to write this into the purchase contract prior to signing. It is an easy inclusion and most sellers of new property will agree to paying the additional cost of the report.

See Appendix D for a more comprehensive list of depreciation rate deductions.

Recently renovated real estate

When a major renovation is conducted on a property, the cost of that renovation is usually a capital expenditure and therefore depreciation can be claimed on that expenditure. This type of renovation is different from conducting a repair to the property, as the cost of a repair is fully tax-deductible in the year of expenditure. The cost of putting in a new kitchen clearly, is not a repair, but it is capital expenditure and therefore should be depreciated, not classed as an expense.

> " Real estate: the tax shelter of the 21st century "

Just like with new construction, it may be possible to negotiate the cost of a Quantity Surveyor's Report into the conditions of sale. This of course will be easier with an 'investor' seller, rather than a 'mum and dad principal place of residence' seller.

Buying second-hand

If you are buying a residential property which is not new and has had previous owners, it is advisable to ask the seller of the property if they ever had a Quantity Surveyor's Report prepared on the property, even if it is not newly renovated and if so, ask for a copy of the report. Clearly this is something you want to do prior to settlement as your seller will not be as keen to talk to you when the deal is done. If no Quantity Surveyor's Report was ever done, you need to do a quick cost-benefit analysis on whether the likely tax-deductions arising from having a Quantity Surveyor's Report completed, will outweigh the cost of the report.

The main factors influencing whether the report would be beneficial or not are the age of the building, and whether any significant renovations have been done within the last five to ten years.

Depreciation + Effective Life Tables

When a depreciating asset is used to produce rental income, you can claim a deduction for its decline in value. There are however different classifications depending on the value of assets.

Purchases under $300

Purchases under $300 in value can be claimed in full in the year of purchase.

Provided the depreciating asset costs less than $300 and is not part of a group of assets that add up to more than $1,000, for example, four components might each cost less than $300 but together they make up, for instance, an airconditioning unit that costs more than $1,000. These assets cannot be counted as individual assets, they must be counted as the whole asset - the air conditioner in this example. If this is not the case, then they may be fully expensed in the year of purchase.

Purchases under $1,000

Purchases under $1,000 in value can be claimed at an accelerated rate of depreciation over four years - by allocating the assets to add in the value pool. The depreciation rate in the first year is 18.75% and 37.5% in subsequent years.

These expenses can be depreciated according to the purchase price and a calculation of their effective life. You can either state the asset's effective life or use the Tax Office's Effective Life Tables for rental properties.

Land

Land is excluded as a depreciating asset because it does not have a limited expected life. Improvements to land or fixtures on land are treated as separate from land and thus, a depreciating asset, regardless of whether the improvement or fixture is removable from the land or permanently attached.

Calculating deductions

Your deduction for the decline in value of a depreciating asset is calculated using either the '**prime cost**' or '**diminishing value method**'. Both methods are based on the effective life of the asset.

Diminishing Value Method

This assumes that the decline in value each year is the constant proportion of the remaining value and reduces progressively over time. The use of this method increases your deduction in the early years, at the expense of reducing your deduction in later years.

$$\frac{\text{Base value} \times (\text{Days held} / 365) \times 200\%}{\text{Asset's effective life}}$$

Prime Cost Method

This assumes that the value of the depreciating asset decreases uniformly over its effective life. The use of this method means that the depreciation deduction is constant over the term of the effective life of the asset.

$$\frac{\text{Assets cost} \times (\text{days held} / 365) \times 100\%}{\text{Asset's effective life}}$$

Effective Life of a Depreciating Asset

This is the length of time that a depreciating asset can be used by an entity for a taxable purpose, or for the purpose of producing income. It takes into account the wear and tear from reasonably expected circumstances of use, assuming reasonable levels of maintenance, and has regard for the period within which it is likely to be scrapped, sold for no more than scrapped value, or abandoned.

Effective life is expressed in years, including fractions of years. It is not rounded to the nearest whole year.

" depreciation is your tax-deduction for not spending any money "

For most depreciating assets, you can either make your own estimate of its effective life or adopt the effective life determined by the tax commissioner.

The ATO Effective Life Tables can be found in Appendix C

These tables are for all freestanding items, sometimes called chattels or fixtures and fittings. 'Freestanding' means items designed to be portable or movable.

Any attachment to the premises is only for the item's temporary stability. 'Fixed' means items annexed or attached by any means, for example screws, nails, bolts, glue, adhesive, grout, or cement, but not merely for temporary stability.

The effective life of items in the Effective Life Tables as set out by the Tax Office, can be revised, provided sufficient evidence can be given to justify the change.

Which method of depreciation should we use?

The selection of the correct depreciation method for you really is a matter of choice.

Obviously, when you compare the 'diminishing value method' with the 'prime cost method', the diminishing value method will give you a much greater deduction in the early years. However, over time this amount of depreciation deduction decreases, whereas the prime cost method might be lower in the first few years, but it remains the same throughout the whole time you own the asset.

If you're looking for ease of calculation, I'd go the prime cost method, as you don't have to recalculate how much you can claim every year.

If you're looking for maximum tax-deductions in the early part of ownership of property, then go the diminishing value method.

When you consider effective life, again it's really a matter of which one suits your circumstances at the time. If you believe the effective life of a particular asset is much shorter than what has been recommended by the Tax Office, and you can justify your rationale, then by all means use the actual effective life of the asset to calculate the appropriate amount of depreciation you believe to be correct.

I personally don't believe that one method is significantly better than the others. It is a matter of choice.

Chapter 8

Getting cash credits for tax on real estate up front

As we have discussed, when you buy an investment property, you get additional deductions which can be offset against the rental property income. When we have a net negative gearing outcome such as the one we are about to describe, the negative gearing effect can be offset against salary and other income.

If no further action is taken, the tax benefit is not received or felt until your Income Tax Return is lodged, in which case you can get the appropriate refund. However, there is a way that you can get this tax benefit throughout the year, and not have to wait until you lodge your tax return to get the additional tax saving. You may as well get the benefit of using the money throughout the year rather than the Tax Office.

Income Tax Variation

By lodging an Income Tax Variation form, you can notify the Tax Office that you expect to have expenses that will reduce your Income Tax liability - such as those resulting from a negatively geared rental property. To do this you:

1. Estimate how much additional tax-deduction you are likely to have throughout the year.
2. Lodge the Income Tax Variation form.
3. The Tax Office notifies your employer of your reduced Income Tax liability and your employer subsequently takes out less tax from your pay packet.

Let me show you how this works:

Example:

$80,000 Salary

Investment Property Purchases	$ 450,000
Purchase Costs	$ 10,000
Rental Income	$ 19,500
Expenses:	
Insurance	$ 650
Rates	$ 1,600
Management Agent (7.5%)	$ 1,463
Body Corporate Fees	$ 1,500
Depreciation	$ 4,500
Interest ($460,000 x 7.5% p/a)	$ 34,500
Total Expenses	$ 44,213
Net Tax Loss p.a.	$ 24,713

Tax Secrets of a Real Estate Millionaire

The final figure above would be the tax loss that is offset against the salary. The result would be as follows:

Example:

Salary	$ 80,000
Less Property Tax Loss	$ 24,713
Taxable Income	**$ 55,287**
Tax on $80,000	$ 17,547
Tax on $55,287	$ 9,515
Net Tax Saving	**$ 8,032**

With this figure you would lodge an Income Tax Variation Request to reduce your taxable income from $80,000 to $55,287.

The Tax Office would then notify the investor's employer to reduce the weekly tax withheld:

Previous Tax withheld	$ 337.00 p/w
Reduced Tax withheld	$ 182.00 p/w
Savings on Tax withheld	**$155.00 p/w**

Note: - Benefit is gained weekly, not in a lump sum when the tax return is lodged.
- Calculations exclude medicare levy

In the end, the real cost to own the property is $16,681 or $320.79 per week.

Example:

Net Tax Loss	$ 24,713
Less Net Tax Savings	$ 8,032
Revised Property Costs	**$ 16,681**
or	$320.79 per week

In this way, you get to utilise the additional cashflow that your investment property is creating throughout the year. You are not giving the Tax Office an interest free loan; instead you get the money you would otherwise be entitled to at the end of the year, on a week by week basis.

BUT REMEMBER NEGATIVE GEARING IS STILL A LOSS, AND MONEY YOU HAVE TO FIND EVERY WEEK!

BUY A POSITIVE OR MANUFACTURED POSITIVE PROPERTY AND IT PUTS MONEY BACK IN YOUR POCKET EVERY WEEK!

So what is rental property income anyway?

Well, apart from the obvious, being the rent received from renting out the investment property, there are a few other categories which may surprise you that are classified as income, and should be included on your Income Tax return.

Rental property income classifications:

- rent received from tenants
- compensation for loss of rent (e.g. an insurance company payment)
- letting or booking fees
- reimbursements or recoupments (e.g. a reimbursement by a tenant for the costs of repairs to a property)
- lease surrender receipts
- lease premium receipts
- bond monies retained to cover repairs or cleaning etc.
- profit from sale of a rental property if bought and sold within a 12 month timeframe (see Chapter 9 - Capital Gains Tax)
- profit from sale of a rental property, if bought and sold over a 12 month timeframe (Note: this profit is considered a capital gain and may be eligible for a 50% Capital Gains Tax discount)

See Chapter 9 for more information on Capital Gains Tax

Depending on whether the landlord is considered to be in business or not, receipts such as those for lease surrender may be ordinary income or capital gain.

Non-income receipts

Bond money lodged by a tenant is not income, so refunds of bond monies cannot be claimed as an expense. If part of the bond is retained for repairs or cleaning, the amount kept must be included as income in the year retained, and a deduction claimed for the expense incurred in the year that it was incurred.

One off tax credit variations

Sometimes an investor may find that in one particular year expenses on a property may be extraordinarily high. There might be a need to do a major repair of the property, or major capital works may need to be undertaken. This would mean that the taxpayer's income for the year, after taking into account real estate offsets such as negative gearing, could be considerably lower than in other years.

In situations such as this, the taxpayer could lodge a one-off Income Tax Variation Request, so that less tax could be taken out in that one particular year by his employer to compensate for the extra expenses incurred during this year of extraordinary circumstances, which would of course be tax-deductible.

"record all information pertaining to a property in an asset register"

When circumstances are returned to normal and the property no longer requires extraordinary expenses, the taxpayer could resume either normal taxation from his salary and wage, or revert back to the normal level of Income Tax variation, to take account of the operational tax loss on his property.

Chapter 9

Tax-free wealth creation

Living the great Australian dream – owning your own home. For many years this has been the only wealth creation strategy of the Australian population. You would work hard to save a deposit and buy a home that you could live in for the next fifty years and raise a family. Your interest and repayments were on the never-never plan, such that you probably paid for the house three times over and hopefully by retirement age you had paid the rotten thing off.

Well times are changing. As a population, we only stay in our home (or our principal place of residence, as we call it, for tax purposes), on average, for seven years before we either change location or upgrade to a bigger, better home until we find ourselves childless and living in a house far too big for our needs. Then we either downsize or move into a retirement village. Does that sound familiar?

Regardless of whether this is your only wealth creation strategy or not, your home or your principal place of residence, is a tax efficient way of accumulating wealth. Let's face it, you have to live somewhere, so you may as well be paying money into your own pockets rather than paying rent to someone else. The big advantage with owning your own home is that any of the gain in value of the property is TAX-FREE.

Historically, over the past 20 years, house prices across metro areas in Australia have increased on average by 7.5% per annum, outpacing the general rate of inflation considerably, which is an average of 3.6%. That means that houses have quadrupled in value over this period of time!

Irrespective of what the historical growth has been in the real estate market in Australia, it would be safe to say prices are going to go up in the future and the cheapest time to enter the property market is now, and any of the expected further growth is better off in your pocket than in the landlords! Why not have that gain, tax-free if you live in the property?

Your principal place of residence

When I was consulting in my accountancy practice, I remember a particular couple who had recently moved to the Sunshine Coast from New Zealand. They were a young

> "your home, or principal place of residence is a tax efficient way of accumulating wealth"

retired couple with lots of energy, get up and go, and a real zest for making money and life in general. They loved gardening, and turning a house into a home, so several years back they took this talent and turned it into tax-free profits.

Tax Secrets of a Real Estate Millionaire

The first home they bought was a brand-new spec home, built by one of the project builders. They purchased the property prior to completion, and asked that only basic landscaping such as driveways and paths be completed. Over the next couple of years they went about establishing gardens, putting in a pool, and basically turning the shell of the house that they had purchased, into a home. Obviously, a couple of years down the track their property was worth more because of the time and effort they had put into improving their home.

They did also experience general capital growth in the area as they were smart in selecting a property which was in Stage 1 of an 11 stage development, with big advertising and marketing dollars behind the development. This meant that their property increased in value simply as a result of the marketing campaign of the developer. These two factors combined, meant that they were able to sell their property a couple of years later for a substantial profit - to the tune of around $250,000.

The couple kept themselves on a relatively tight but comfortable budget, and had worked out they needed $50,000 a year to cover their lifestyle in retirement.

> "turn your lifestyle into a business, save yourself some tax, make yourself some money and have a good time doing it"

On the sale of their home they replaced their reserves, or savings, with $100,000, being their living expenses over the past two years. The $250,000 gain that they made on the sale of their home was of course tax-free, as profits made on the sale of your principal place of residence are tax-free.

The couple then had an extra $150,000 in the kitty to reenter the market and do it again. They reentered in Stage 3 of the eight staged development. They recontracted the same project builder who had built their first home. They modified their original plans slightly to reflect improvements to suit their lifestyle, which they clearly recognised from living in the previous house design for those two years. Again they elected to have only minor landscaping completed by their builder, and again they set about turning their shell of a house into a home.

Within about 18 months, they had done all they could in the way of furnishing, landscaping and gardening and decided they were bored and needed to move on to a new project. Well, what do you know? The weight of the developer's advertising and marketing budget had again pushed the value of their property higher. Their improvements and homemaking meant that their home was again worth about $200,000 more than it had cost them.

As previously, they took out their living expenses over the past 18 months totalling $75,000 and replaced their kitty. The remaining $125,000 was put back into consolidated revenue/savings, tax-free. In effect, this motivated, retired couple had gained 5½ years worth of living expenses by being sensible, tax efficient and proactive, just by doing what they loved - primarily gardening.

The couple decided to purchase another block of land at this time to build what they considered their dream home, but also to use some of the money they had made and take a six-month trip around Australia, something they had dreamed of doing for many years. No doubt, on their return the couple would have started all over again.

Interestingly, I spoke to them before they left about the possibility of them writing a journal of their travels as a sort of self-help guide for retirees on a budget doing a simple trip. They knew of course, what this would have meant for them tax-wise. If they proceeded to write the journal or book on their return and publish it for sale, a great percentage of their expenses related to their trip around Australia would have been tax-deductible against the income received from the sale of the book.

See how it all starts to fit into place, and by being a little bit savvy, means you really can turn your lifestyle into a business, save yourself some tax, make yourself some money and have a really good time doing it.

Dangers of trading in your principal place of residence

There are some dangers associated with the strategy that was employed by my motivated retirees above. That is, if the Tax Office deems you to be in the business of 'trading' in your principal place of residence, they can not only go back and reassess previous tax returns, but they can charge you fines and penalty interest on any tax that they deem you should have paid on the profit from the sale of your principal place of residence which would have otherwise been tax-free.

Whoa! What do I mean by that, you may ask?

Well, basically, if the Tax Office sees that you are buying and selling and making a profit on your principal place of residence within short succession, they will deem you to be in the business of trading in your principal place of residence, and therefore tax you on any of the profits you make as a result.

I guess the real question is: "What defines trading in your principal place of residence?" and "What defines moving from one residence to another for private reasons and is there a specified timeframe for that happening?"

Firstly, let's deal with the definition of trading in your principal place of residence. The Tax Office has not laid down guidelines which specifically say 'x' period of time is considered appropriate to own a property that you live in before selling it at a profit. Nor has it indicated how much of a profit you are able to make on a principal place of residence before tax could be deemed payable.

Secondly, the Tax Office has not specifically outlined what private reasons could be considered reasonable for selling a property at a profit.

Tax Secrets of a Real Estate Millionaire

So what's the poor "mum and dad" property owner or motivated retirees meant to do? Well that's a tricky one. I've known homeowners to sell a property because after purchasing it they find they don't like the next-door neighbours, or someone in the family is allergic to the Jacaranda tree in the backyard, or the soil isn't fertile enough to grow vegies in, or they wanted to live closer to the family. Subsequently they turn around and sell property in relatively quick succession and make a profit on the deal. There is nothing wrong with any of these situations, and profits, rightly, should be tax-free.

The real area of doubt comes when this practice happens over and over again, because it is then that the Tax Office has justification for querying a homeowner's real intent for selling a particular property. Was the decision-making process motivated by profit or was the decision motivated by some other private reason?

If you are someone who has bought and sold your principal place of residence a number of times in quick succession, or you know of someone who has, I highly recommend you make an appointment with your accountant and tax adviser sooner rather than later, and discuss your personal circumstances and any potential tax risk with them.

If the buying and selling of the principal place of residence incorporated actually building a new residence, not just renovating an old one, then not only could you be up for additional Capital Gains Tax on the profits, plus back taxes and penalties over previous years, but the homeowner could also be up for GST on the sale price of the properties as well. Now that's when it really starts to get nasty.

See my chapter on GST and new residential property later in this book.

If at some point a home owner decides that he or she is on a pretty good wicket and likes making money out of improving their principal place of residence, and wants to turn the process into a business, they should then look at setting up a structure from which to run the business.

Chapter 10

Investor versus Trader

There are subtle differences that can make one strategy much better than the other, just in the way your business is structured. At this point, I think it's appropriate to discuss the difference between being an investor and being in the business of real estate (being a trader or dealer).

Whether you are an investor or a trader can have very different tax implications, but first you need to define which one it is that you are.

Tax Secrets of a Real Estate Millionaire

Investor

An investor will generally purchase properties for long-term investment purposes, generating an income through rent or an eventual capital gain. They hold on to their real estate for prolonged periods of time and only make a few real estate transactions every year.

You are defined as an investor if:

- You purchase real estate as an investment from which to produce income through rent or capital gain.

- You improve real estate in order to take advantage of increased equity rather than for resale.

- You produce income through rent rather than resale.

- Your real estate sales or purchases are few or irregular.

- You hold real estate for long periods of time.

- You don't generate income solely from buying and selling real estate.

Tax benefits for the investor

- Any profits made from the sale of a property after 12 months of ownership will be concessionally taxed as a result of the 50% Capital Gains Tax exemption.

- Expenses relating to the operation of the investment will be tax-deductible.

- For financing and refinancing your assets will be treated as long-term assets and loan to valuation ratios (LVR) may be higher. This means investors may potentially be able to borrow more as the financial institutions expect the investor to hold the assets over a longer term.

Trader/dealer

A trader/dealer will be the opposite. They will purchase real estate with the purpose of developing, subdividing, strata titling or improving the property, or to onsell the property quickly to another purchaser for an immediate gain. They dedicate most of their time to seeking out or developing properties and the majority of their income will be attributed to these activities.

You are defined as a trader if:

- You are purchasing or selling large quantities of real estate.

- Spending most of your time sourcing, purchasing or developing real estate.

- The majority of your income is generated through real estate development and sales.

- You buy real estate with the intention of subdividing, constructing or improving homes to sell.

- You maintain staff to facilitate sales or improve real estate purchased.

- You turn over properties frequently and quickly.

Tax benefits for the trader

- Whilst the profit on sale of any property held for greater than 12 months will not be entitled to 50% Capital Gains Tax exemption, any expenses related to the acquisition, purchase or operation of the property will be fully tax-deductible.

- The costs associated with finding and acquiring the property would not be considered a capital cost and will be fully deductible against operational income.

- All associated expenses with running the business such as motor vehicles, home office, staff, consultants etc., would all be fully tax-deductible.

- Any GST credits for running the business could be offset against the GST payable on the sales made via the business, i.e. the sale of real estate.

Can you be both a trader and an investor?

Yes, you can have properties that you keep for the long term and rent or improve and allow to appreciate in value, while you purchase others with the intention of turning them over quickly and taking advantage of immediate gains.

The important thing is to keep these different types of property investment segregated in your portfolio so that you can take advantage of the different tax benefits that apply to each. You should consider owning the investments you intend to keep long-term in separate legal entities from the properties you intend to turn over quickly for a profit.

This way the structures that hold your long-term assets would typically not be registered for the GST unless the property owned is commercial and turning over more than $75,000. The structures that are in the business of trading in real estate at a profit would be registered for GST and would be set up to claim all of your operational expenses associated with running a business against the profit that the business earns. I call this trust a 'flipper trust'. Your structure would look something like the following diagram.

Tax Secrets of a Real Estate Millionaire

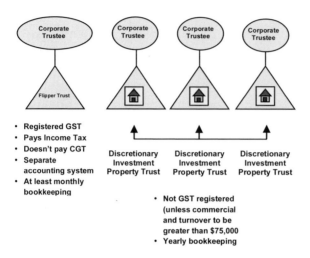

Investment Trust Structure

- Registered GST
- Pays Income Tax
- Doesn't pay CGT
- Separate accounting system
- At least monthly bookkeeping

- Not GST registered (unless commercial and turnover to be greater than $75,000
- Yearly bookkeeping

When you get down the track a bit

As you acquire more investment properties you will inevitably get annoyed at having a separate bank account for every trust – not to mention the additional bank fees. Whilst this is better and easier for accounting purposes as it keeps the income and expenses for each property completely separate and identifiable, it can get cumbersome.

At this stage, it is probably time for you to have an 'admin trust'. This is not an asset protection vehicle, it is more of an accounting vehicle. The admin trust would have the bank account and receive all the rent from all the investment properties and would pay all the expenses for all the investment properties, including interest.

From an accounting perspective having the admin trust means you now have to keep a full accounting system and update it at least monthly, if not weekly. You need to be able to code every rent cheque and every expense to each property. Conversely, when you are accounting for each individual trust through their own bank account, a once a year bank reconciliation and summary is normally sufficient.

Just like the admin trust, the flipper trust will also need a full accounting system and book keeping.

The admin trust structure might look something like this.

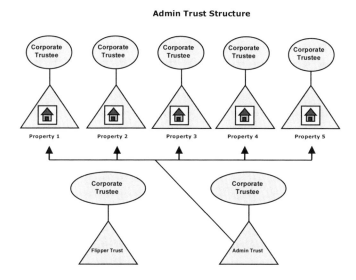

Admin Trust Structure

Wrapping

One strategy that has become particularly popular over the last 5 to 10 years is a strategy commonly called 'wrapping'. This common name is not quite accurate as there are a number of different types or contracts and styles of investing in this category, and better terminology would actually be 'vendor financing', or 'lease optioning' or 'rent to buy'. But so as not to complicate things I will refer to them as wrap deals.

You may ask; "Why am I talking about this kind of deal in a tax book, isn't this a property strategy?" Well, the reason behind this is that wrap properties are treated as trading stock, therefore the income earned, both on the backend profit and the positive cash flow per month, is treated as ordinary income.

Tax Secrets of a Real Estate Millionaire

Having the income treated as ordinary income will also mean that any expenses related to earning that income will all be fully tax-deductible against the income. Expenses incurred whilst searching for a property, negotiating with agents, travelling to open a property for viewing, would all be examples of fully deductible expenditure against the wrap income.

Wrapping is a strategy that renders assessable income, not as capital gains, but ordinary income. Those individuals, companies or other structures who earn their income through wrapping, would be treated as traders or dealers, or in the business of real estate. This means of course, that any expenditure directly associated with the income earned from running the business of wrapping, will be tax-deductible.

Those in the game tend to have other names for the strategy such as; vendor financing, lease options or even instalment contracts. Whilst all these names refer basically to the same thing, they actually have quite different tax consequences.

Let's first look at what wrapping actually means.

Wrapping a property is the process of buying a property, usually significantly under market value; sometimes fixing it up (more often than not), and then selling the property to another party who would not normally be able to borrow the money from conventional lenders to buy the property.

You may well ask; "How does the seller get his money?" Well, the seller actually loans the incoming buyer the money, but the title on the property doesn't transfer to the new incoming buyer until such time as he is able to pay the full amount of the purchase price.

Let me walk you through a real example that a friend of mine did in Caboolture, Queensland:

My friend purchased a property in Caboolture for $112,000 years ago. He was a smart negotiator and used a strategy I call the 'scatter technique' to purchase the property. The real value of the property, which was confirmed by a bank valuation, was $135,000 at the time (today the property is probably worth $320,000).

Because the property was purchased clearly under market value, the property was able to be refinanced immediately on a loan at 80% of $135,000 ($108,000). This meant my friend's total outlay on the property was just $4,000 (plus costs).

He put a little advertisement in the newspaper - 3 lines and he received 60 calls. He found a couple who had had a bad experience with banks previously. They had a bit of a mark on their CRAA or credit rating from something that had happened a couple of years earlier and consequently were not in a position to borrow through the normal banking channels.

They did however have a deposit ready of $15,000 which they paid to my friend. At this point my friend is now $11,000 (the deposit less purchasing costs) better off in his pocket. He on-sold the property under a wrap contract, or more precisely, rent to buy or lease to buy contract, for $150,000. This meant the new purchaser coming in still had $135,000 left to pay on his vendor financing loan. Let me show you how the figures worked out:

Example:

Caboolture
4Br, 1 bath LUG, 650m2 block

Purchased	$ 112,000
Revalue	$ 135,000
(80% loan = $108,000)	
Deposit Paid	$ 12,000

Advertisement placed in paper – 60 calls

Sold	$150,000
Wrap deposit taken	$ 15,000

Tax Secrets of a Real Estate Millionaire

Now remember, I said the property actually doesn't change hands from a title perspective. This means my friend still legally owns the property and therefore still holds a mortgage on the property of $108,000. He does however have a contract which is legally binding and unconditional, to sell that property to the new owners at an agreed price of $150,000 less the $15,000 deposit which he has already collected. Incidentally, the $15,000 deposit was immediately released to my friend for use - not held in trust for years and years.

The repayments the new owner made to my friend were effectively loan repayments or rent with the option to purchase or lease to buy on the property on his outstanding amount of $135,000.

This is how the numbers panned out:

Example:

Profit upfront	$11,000 (less costs)
The new owner's loan was at a vendor finance rate of which equated to	$135,000 8.57% $964 /month
My friend's loan was for at bank rate of which equated to	$108,000 5.97% $537 /month
Positive Cash Flow per month	$427 /month
Profit on refinance by buyer	$27,000

This obviously meant that my friend now had a **positive cash flow** of $427 per month. Plus he was guaranteed a profit at what we call the 'backend' of the deal, of $27,000 when the property was eventually either sold or refinanced.

Now, we're not necessarily talking about little cruddy old houses either. This is a picture of the actual house my friend purchased:

Now, you may be wondering, why on earth would anyone buy a house for $150,000 when it's only worth $135,000? To answer this you have got to remember that these people wouldn't have been able to buy a house otherwise, or at least that's what they believed. This was an opportunity to buy a house in an area they believed would have more growth, plus the ability to be able to add an extension to the house, fix it up, repaint it, put in a new kitchen, do anything they wanted to the house as if it were their own (because it is their own). This meant that they would be able to either refinance or sell the property, probably relatively quickly, if they chose to. They would certainly have the opportunity to bring the house up to at least the $150,000 and potentially more.

Let's have a quick look at what type of people might be looking for a wrap style deal.

What type of person does 'Wraps' suit?

- Self employed with low taxable income
- New business owners
- New migrants
- Those with CRAA issues
- Those with mainly Social Security incomes
- Young people needing a kick start

- Those who have trouble saving
- Ex-bankrupts
- New divorcees starting over

Conversely, the types of people who would be interested in owning a wrap property would include the following types of investors.

Who do 'Wraps' suit as a 'Wrapper'?

- Investors seeking strong cash flow
- Investors prepared to actively manage their wrappees – especially in the beginning
- Need to have a strong personality

Possible wrap outcomes

With a wrap property there are really only three possible outcomes:

1. They stay and pay
2. They refinance or sell
3. They don't pay and you have to EVICT

Types of wraps

There are three types of wrap contracts;

1. An instalment contract or vendor financing contract
2. A 'rent to buy' or 'lease to purchase' contract and
3. A lease option contract

Instalment Contracts or Vendor Financing contracts

An instalment contract or a vendor financing contract has never really been very popular in Australia, certainly not as popular as it is in the United States. The reason behind this is because of our Capital Gains Tax laws. The property is effectively, sold immediately. Then just like a bank finance contract, the investor takes a mortgage over the property and vendor finances the new buyer into the deal.

This means that Capital Gains Tax will be payable immediately because the sale has taken place, even though our investor hasn't actually received the money for the sale. You can see why this type of contract isn't popular amongst investors. Legislation on instalment contracts does vary from state to state, but the taxation implication does not.

Rent/Lease to Buy Purchasing

A 'rent to buy', or 'lease to purchase' contract means that part of the rent being paid by the potential new purchaser is being set aside as a partial down payment on the property. Typically these contracts might be two years or five years in length. It's basically like a mandatory savings plan with the right to purchase the property at an agreed value within a specified timeframe.

These contracts can be quite complicated and typically suit properties in medium to high growth areas. The future profits for the investor are locked in, and sometimes the proportional option fee is scaled in accordance with how long the option contract exists before being exercised.

From a tax perspective, the positive cash flow is clearly income, but for Capital Gains Tax purposes, a sale does not take place until the option contract is exercised. These styles of contracts are popular with some investors, but most tend to find them too complicated to understand and explain to a potential buyer or wrappee.

Lease Option Contracts

Lease option contracts are certainly the most popular and probably suit the Australian Tax Laws the best. They basically have rental payments that mirror image standard principal and interest loan repayments within the first five years. Most contracts range from two to five years and have a provision that any maintenance issues are dealt with by the tenant/potential buyer.

Backend profits or refinance profits are locked in and will be counted as a sale for Capital Gains Tax purposes when the refinance and/or sale of the property takes place.

When it comes to any form of wrap, my personal preference is to own the property long-term as I believe in the long-term the cash flow will outstrip the short-term extra cash flow you might be making on a wrap, and the long-term growth on the property will far outweigh the short-term backend profit locked in under the contract. However, you must remember that when it comes to investing, I have a motto that I live by:

My Motto:

Real wealth comes from accumulation not trading!!!!

Trader/dealer expenses

When you are in business, any of your operational expenses associated with your business will be tax–deductible. This means any expenses that you need to incur to run the business will be a direct tax-deduction against the income of your business. So if you are in the business of trading in real estate, any expenses you need to incur to run this business will be tax-deductible against the profits you make from selling your trading stock – which in this case is real estate.

Let's go through some of the more common expenses which would now be tax-deductible to your real estate trading business.

Car expenses and substantiation

There are four different methods of substantiating car expense claims. The requirements for each method are different, resulting in higher or lower claims depending on which method is used. A taxpayer must generally choose one of the following methods, unless an exemption applies:

1. Cents per kilometre method
2. 12% of original value method
3. 1/3 of actual expenses method
4. Log book method

The rules apply to most motor vehicles as well as vehicles that carry a load of less than one tonne or less than nine passengers. A taxpayer can choose only one of the four methods for each car in an income year to claim the expenses, and of course, it is advantageous to choose the method which gives the highest claim. The method chosen can be changed, as long as the taxpayer is entitled to claim deductions under this alternative method. Let us look at some examples using these methods:

Cents per km method

With this method, the taxpayer does not need to substantiate any of these car expenses. The car expenses are determined by the business kilometres travelled during that income year.

The maximum kilometres that can be claimed per car is 5,000. This should be based on a reasonable estimate, as no documentation needs to be kept with this method.

The claim is calculated as follows:

Business km travelled (limited to 5,000km in the income year) × Rate based on engine capacity

Cents per Km method[2]		
Engine Capacity		**Cents per Kilometre**
Ordinary Car	**Rotary Engine**	**2013/14 Income year**
Up to 1.6 litre	Up to 0.8 litre	63 cents
1.601 litre - 2.6 litre	0.801 litre - 1.3 litre	74 cents
Over 2.601 litre	Over 1.301 litre	75 cents

This method can also be used for 2 or more taxpayers who own the same car, both of whom use it separately for business purposes. Each taxpayer is entitled to use this method to claim their separate deductions.

12% of original value method

With this method, car expenses do not need to be substantiated, but the method can only be used if the car has travelled more than 5,000 kilometres in the course of doing business.

The taxpayer can claim 12% of the cost of the car upon purchasing or leasing, up to that vehicle's depreciation limit. If the owner is registered for GST, they may also be able to claim input credits.

---

[2] Australian Tax Office, *Claiming a deduction for car expenses using the cents per kilometre method.* http://www.ato.gov.au

1/3 of actual expenses method

The 1/3 of actual expenses method is based on the *actual* business kilometres exceeding 5,000 kilometres in an income year.

With this method 1/3 of the car expenses, including operational expenses and depreciation, can be claimed by the taxpayer as long as those expenses can be substantiated. Luxury leased vehicle expenses cannot be deducted using this method. Deductions are limited to depreciation and finance charges.

It is not necessary to substantiate fuel and oil expenses providing the expenses are based on a reasonable estimate of the kilometres travelled.

Log Book method

For the log book method, the car must be either owned or leased by the taxpayer and can be used whether the vehicle travels 5,000 kilometres or not.

All of the car's expenses must be substantiated by the taxpayer if using this method, including registration, insurance, repairs, services, fuel, depreciation and leasing charges.

When using the log book method, the taxpayer must keep a log book through which the deductions are determined by calculating the percentage of travel which is business related:

$$\frac{\text{Business km}}{\text{Total kms}} \times \text{Total Car Expenses}$$

Keeping a log book

A log book must be maintained for a continuous 12 week period in an income year, in that first year of business. The taxpayer can choose the timeframe in which the log book is to be recorded providing the weeks are consecutive. If claiming for more than one car, the log books for the individual cars must be recorded in the same 12 week period. This only needs to be done once every 5 years unless a notification is sent from the Tax Office, or you acquire a second car or the percentage of your claim has changed.

The log book must record all relevant information related to the journeys, including but not exclusive to, when the period starts and ends, total kilometres travelled, the business percentage, where the trip was made to and the various odometer readings related to all of these trips.

To see a comparison summary of car expense calculation methods see Appendix I.

Home Office expenses

Home office expenses can be made if the taxpayer can substantiate that part of the home is being used for business purposes without being an actual place of business. The expenses can be claimed as either the actual expenditure or an estimated expenditure, in which case a diary will need to be kept for a four week period to record the pattern of expenses so the home office percentage can be calculated. This will need to be done every year.

Expenses which can be included are running expenses of the home office such as electricity, gas, office furniture depreciation and other expenses incurred during the course of business. Telephone expenses identified from the phone bill as business expenses, are also deductible, as are expenses such as rent, rates and home insurance. When operating from a principal place of residence, care must be given when claiming these expenses as it may affect exemption from Capital Gains Tax if the home from which the home office is running, is later sold.

Claiming the cost of travel expenses

Most investors get confused about when travel expenses can be claimed as a tax-deduction. These expenses can be broken down into two categories; pre-property purchase and post-property purchase.

Pre-property purchase

You cannot claim the cost of travelling to search for a property to buy. These expenses are essentially capital, and therefore are not deductible, and they are also not included in the assets cost base for Capital Gains Tax purposes. These expenses cannot be used for any part of a capital works claim either.

Post-property purchase

Once the property is purchased and is income producing, travel expenses incurred whilst inspecting the property or conducting repairs, collecting rent or negotiating with managing agents will all be tax-deductible. If your property happens to also be in a place where you choose to have holidays, and your property inspection coincides with a family holiday, then only the incidental costs to inspect the property are tax-deductible.

Tax Secrets of a Real Estate Millionaire

Travel Deductibility Flow Chart for Real Estate Business Owner

When investors make the leap between being a real estate investor and running a real estate investment business, their real estate investment business starts to be treated like any other business, where the parading expenses of the business are all tax-deductible. I mentioned this here, because as a serious investor running a real estate investment business, you would also be entitled to claim travel allowances for your employees, even when you are the employee yourself.

This possibility starts to become very exciting and I have outlined in Appendix B the travel allowance guidelines for businesses.

TAX ALERTS

Travelling deductions being wasted!!!

This is a very interesting piece of the Australian Taxation Legislation and one that gets overlooked – much to the detriment of taxpayers.

People often travel as part of their business activities including the business of being a real estate investment business. The following rules apply when claiming for business travel expenses incurred inside or outside Australia. These rules apply to self-employed persons, partners and employees alike.

All taxpayers, except employees who receive an allowance from their employer, must obtain documentary evidence of their business travel expenses if they are away from their ordinary residence for 1 night or more. If the person is away from their ordinary residence, either overseas or domestically, for 6 nights or more, additional records must be maintained.

Travel Allowances versus Travel Expenses

The Australian Taxation Office requires that the following information be recorded in a diary or similar document:

- the nature of the activity
- the day and approximate time that the activity began
- how long the activity lasted, and
- where the activity was engaged

Only business activities need be recorded in the diary. However, (and this is where things really start to get interesting), **no written evidence** and **no travel records** are required for travel within Australia if the employee receives a **travel allowance** and claims no more than the amount considered reasonable by the Tax Office.

Think about that! If you are away from home on business overnight, you are able to claim a deduction for a travel allowance in your Company without the need for substantiation, provided the claim does not exceed the amounts stipulated by the Tax Office.

Reasonable amounts are determined by the Australian Taxation Office and are the maximum claims that can be made **without the need for written evidence.**

Claims up to the reasonable amounts limit are allowed without receipts or other written documentary evidence, but only if an allowance was received from the employer. If no allowance was received, or a higher claim is made, then all expenses must be substantiated.

The reasonable amounts limit is tied to the employee's salary level. Therefore, a record must be maintained of the salary level of the employee at the date the travel is undertaken.

This is an incentive for persons operating companies to pay their travel expenses as an allowance to themselves as employees of the company.

Under these rules, it is the expenditure that must not exceed what the Tax Office considers reasonable. This means that employers can pay higher allowances to their employees and the substantiation exemption will still apply, provided the employee's claim is limited to the 'reasonable amount' and the amount paid as an allowance is bona fide and paid to cover specific travel in performing duties as an employee.

Travel expenses do not include motor vehicle expenses, however, taxi fares (or similar expenses) and motor vehicle expenses are treated as travel expenses if they relate to overseas travel. As a general rule, an allowance is treated as being for travel if the period away does not exceed 21 days. For longer periods, the payment may become a living away from home allowance.

See Travel Claims within Australia for reasonable limits chart in Appendix J.

Verification

In some circumstances, the Tax Office may still require an employee to show that they are entitled to the substantiation exception, the reasonable rate used, and the entitlement to a deduction as outlined in this section of the Act. That could mean showing that actual work related travel was undertaken, a bona fide travel allowance was paid, the claim is below the reasonable amount for the destination and that commercial accommodation was used.

The nature and degree of evidence required will depend on the circumstances, e.g. the circumstances under which the employer pays allowances, as well as the occupation of the employee and the total amount of allowances received and claimed during the year.

Tax Return

Neither the allowance nor the expenses have to be included in the employee's tax return if the allowance does not exceed the reasonable amounts and has been fully expended on the deductible expenses. If an amount less than the allowance has been expended, then the employee's Income Tax return must include the allowance and the expenses claimed. If a deduction is claimed, then the allowance must be included in the tax return.

Similar substantiation exceptions exist for international travel, so speak to your accountant about these if you travel overseas for business purposes.

Chapter 11

The tax that gets you when you sell!

Capital Gains Tax and real estate

An investor is liable for Capital Gains Tax if a rental property that has been acquired after the 19 September 1985, is sold, and the proceeds exceed its cost base.

The cost base of the rental property is calculated as follows:

- the purchase price of the property

- incidental costs involved in purchasing the property (these incidental costs would include expenses such as valuation fees, Stamp Duty, remuneration for professional services, transfer costs, advertising etc.)

- other costs incurred in owning the property which have not been deducted previously

- capital expenditure or improvements to the property which have not been expensed as a repair

- capital expenditure to establish, preserve or defend the title to the investment property

Example:

Property Sale Price	$ 300,000
Property Purchase Price	$ 180,000
Stamp Duty	$ 8,975
Agent Sales Commission	$ 10,000
Legal Fees - Purchasing	$ 1,200
Legal Fees – Selling	$ 1,200
Total Costs	$ 201,375
Capital Gain	$ 98,625

Two methods for calculating Capital Gains Tax

There are two methods for calculating Capital Gains Tax; the indexation method and the 50% discount method.

50% Discount Method

To be eligible for the 50% discount on Capital Gains Tax the investor must have owned the property for more than 12 months. The 50% discount is applied to the profit margin between what a property is sold for and the calculated cost base.

For example, on the above calculations, under the 50% discount method the taxpayer would pay tax on half of the $98,625 profit i.e. $49,313.

Indexation Method

The indexation method takes into account the CPI increase in the cost base of the property. The Tax Office has laid out indexation standard factors for each quarter since Capital Gains Tax was first legislated in September 1985. Basically, the Tax Office allows for the inflation effect on the increased value of your property. To this end, I have included the Tax Office indexation method and formula in Appendix E.

See Appendix E for Indexation Tables

The Tax Office made another change in September 1999 which basically made the indexation method obsolete. It effectively froze any cost based indexation as at 30 September 1999 and is only available to purchases obtained prior to this date, and held for at least 12 months prior to this date.

The taxpayer can choose between the 50% discount method or the indexation method. Given the property price boom that we have experienced since the year 2000, it is in most people's interest not to choose the indexation method but instead work out the Capital Gains Tax based on the 50% discount method. It is for this reason that I have focused on the discount method.

17 Essential Capital Gains Tax tips

1. Paper Work can save you Dollars!

Keep records of every circumstance or event that may be relevant to working out capital gains or losses. In all my years as an accountant, seeing clients year after year, the biggest waste of money came from clients not keeping enough reliable evidence to support valid deductions.

Tax Secrets of a Real Estate Millionaire

When it comes to property ownership - records must be kept for 5 years after the relevant time associated with the property. This means for 5 years after you sell a property. If you hold a property for 10 years, you have to keep all the records associated with the property from the time of purchase to 5 years after you sell it.

Also keep records of other tax matters besides Capital Gains Tax (e.g. capital allowance claims, depreciation and GST matters) as these can also be relevant in calculating capital gains or losses.

"Tax deferral catches up with you eventually"

The best way to do this is to record all information pertaining to a property in an Asset Register, and keep copies of all documents such as renovation receipts, purchase statements, loan costs etc., with your Asset Register.

See my website for the 'Asset and Ownership Register'.

www.dymphnaboholt.com.au

2. Planning the right time to sell

If possible, plan to sell your property in the year when your Income Tax from other sources is lowest. Even consider delaying transactions in one tax year and entering into them in the next tax year to defer or lower your total tax bill.

If a capital gain is made in one year, consider liquidating assets which might realise a capital loss

"Plan the right time to sell"

as the capital gains from one asset can be offset against the capital losses of another.

Tax Secrets of a Real Estate Millionaire

For example, if you sell property that has a capital gain and you also own some shares which may have gone down in value, you may wish to sell the shares in the same year as you sell the property, and offset the gains from the real estate against the capital losses from the share portfolio. Even if your investment decision is to hold onto the shares for the long term, you can simply buy the shares back at the low cost base and defer your Income Tax liability to future years when your Income Tax rate might be lower.

By deferring your tax liability in this way, you get to use the Tax Office's money for a longer time interest free! Additionally, with the use of superannuation, you may even be able to defer and reduce the tax liability.

3. Who owns the property can make a big difference!

Not all owners are treated the same for tax purposes. If you own an investment property either as an individual, a trust or in a complying superannuation fund, you are entitled to the concessional Capital Gains Tax treatment. This means you are entitled to the 50% Capital Gains Tax exemption. Companies on the other hand, are not entitled to the 50% Capital Gains Tax exemption and pay tax at the company tax rate on the total amount of profit made from a sale.

> "You don't get a Capital Gains Exemption if you are investing as a company"

Where Capital Gains Tax assessable assets are owned by an individual, discretionary trust or complying superannuation fund, consider holding them for at least 12 months, so that the Capital Gains Tax discount can be used on sale.

Unit trusts on the other hand are fixed trusts and are mostly treated the some as companies for Capital Gains Tax purposes, and would not be entitled to the 50% exemption.

4. You don't get the discount if you are trading

The 50% Capital Gains Tax exemption does not apply to entities that are in the business of trading real estate. When in the business of trading, or buying and selling at a profit, real estate properties are considered trading stock and will not be eligible for the 50% Capital Gains Tax exemption. Any profits made from the sale of these properties will be treated as ordinary income, and taxed accordingly.

5. Tax deferral catches up with you eventually

When disposing of a rental property it is necessary to account separately for depreciating assets sold with the property. These assets when used solely for income producing purposes are subject to a separate balancing adjustment and do not come under the Capital Gains Tax legislation. Any profits or losses made from the sale of these items will be assessed as ordinary income or losses.

6. Contract date to contract date - not settlement date to settlement date!

To qualify for the 50% Capital Gains Tax exemption an investor must hold the property for a period of 12 months. Ironically, the 12 months does not go from settlement date to settlement date. It is calculated from contract date to contract date. This means that the time between the date you sign your original purchase contract to the date you sign a contract to sell must be **over** 12 months i.e. 12 months and one day, in order to get the 50% exemption.

7. Principal place of residency exemption

A principal place of residence (PPR) is exempt from Capital Gains Tax. The definition of a home can include a house, cottage, unit, retirement unit, caravan, houseboat or even a mobile home. However in this country, you are only allowed one principal place of residence, unlike in other countries like the United States where you can own multiple.

8. The Six-Year-Rule

If an investor initially lives in their nominated home as their principal place of residence, but for whatever reason chooses to leave the property and rent it out for a period of time, they can still maintain that property was their principal place of residence and therefore the property remains exempt from Capital Gains Tax, for a period of up to six years, provided they do not have another nominated principal place of residence during that time. It is irrelevant whether that property is used as a rental property during the six-year timeframe. This section of legislation is commonly known as the **six-year-rule**.

The six-year-rule can be extended for another six years every time the owners move back into the property and reclaim it as their principal place of residence. Remember, the six-year rule can only continue to apply if the owner does not have another nominated principal place of residence.

9. The six month transitional rule

When you change one principal place of residence for another, by either selling one and buying another or by changing your previous principal place of residence to an investment property and acquiring another, you can only hold both of the properties as your principal place of residence for a period of up to six months. This is called the 'transition' phase. Other than during this transition phase, you are only allowed to have one principal place of residence at any one time.

If you decide to keep your previous principal place of residence as an investment property, it is prudent to have the property valued at the time of change as capital gains will start to be taxable from that time and therefore calculated from that valuation onwards.

10. Home business tax-deductions catches you when you sell!

When you run a business from home, you are entitled to claim part of the costs of owning the home as a tax-deduction against the business. Conversely, when that property is sold – part of the sale profits will be subject to Capital Gains Tax. Clearly, this can be a double edged sword.

11. Size is important!

The exemption for Capital Gains Tax for a principal place of residence is restricted to properties of a maximum land area size of 5 acres or 2 hectares. Sellers of acreage properties will therefore have to pay Capital Gains Tax on profit made from the remainder of their land. Commercially viable acreage also may be able to be sold as a going concern.

12. On the wrong side on the law; ignorance is not an excuse.

Some taxpayers, often through ignorance, find themselves on the wrong side of the law and facing severe tax penalties and back taxes, by trading in principal places of residence. What does this mean? Well, particularly in recent years, with the popularity of TV renovating and home improvement shows, and the growth in the property market, many home owners have jumped on the bandwagon. They have either bought older homes, done them up and sold them at a profit, or built new homes, established them and sold them at a profit.

Whilst on the face of it there is nothing wrong with this, if you make a habit of it and do a number of these principal place of residence profit ventures in succession, it would be reasonable that the Tax Office could deem you to be in the business of trading in your principal place of residence. Therefore, the profits you have made on your previous transaction should have had Capital Gains Tax paid on them. Believe me, such an unexpected tax bill with penalties is not only a rude awakening, it may leave the taxpayer in financial difficulty if the money is not easily available to pay the tax bill.

The introduction of self-assessment of our tax returns meant lodging our tax returns became more efficient. However on the flip side, it also meant more resources were put into auditing tax returns and taxpayer's actions. The onus for 'getting it right' is squarely on the taxpayer's shoulders.

13. What if I inherit great Aunt Bertha's house?

The main issue when it comes to inherited property and Capital Gains Tax depends on whether the house was originally purchased by the deceased pre-20 September 1985 or post-20 September 1985. This will determine the acquired date for the person who inherits it. These critical dates are the dates when Capital Gains Tax was introduced into Australia and amended.

> " If an inherited property is sold within 2 years after acquisition than the property is exempt from Capital Gains Tax"

Pre-CGT property

Pre-CGT property left to a beneficiary in a Will is deemed to have been acquired on date of death of the deceased at market value.

Note: If the property sold within 2 years of great Aunt Bertha's death then the property is exempt from Capital Gains Tax. This one little piece of knowledge could save you thousands, or cost you thousands if you ignorantly didn't get around to selling great Aunt Bertha's house for a couple of years and then find yourself with a tax bill that could have easily been avoided.

Post-CGT property

Post-CGT property left to a beneficiary in a Will is deemed to have been acquired on the same date that the deceased acquired it.

Note: If however, the property was Great Aunt Bertha's principal place of residence and not an investment property, then her ownership would be exempt up until her death and would then start to be assessable for Capital Gains Tax from when it passed to you upon her death.

14. Joint Tenants and Tenants-in-Common

What's the difference?

Joint Tenants

Joint Tenants is when an asset is owned equally in joint names and all owners must be involved with all dealings with the asset e.g. sale, mortgage, income, liability etc. On the death of one of the owners, the asset can be transferred to the surviving owner regardless of the contents of a Will.

This situation normally occurs in family or marital relationships where an asset can be owned in more than one individual's name. In the case of the death of a joint tenant, the deceased person's interest in a property passes to the survivor by operation of law. The survivor is deemed to have acquired the property on the same date the deceased acquired it for Capital Gains Tax purposes.

Tenants-in-Common

Tenants-in-Common is when an asset is owned in fixed proportions and can be dealt with by any proportional owner to the extent of their proportional ownership. E.g. one owner may choose to sell only their percentage of ownership in an asset. On death, the owner's proportional ownership is treated as part of the estate and dealt with in accordance with the Will.

When dealing with assets held as Tenants-in-Common it is important to realise borrowings against the asset can only be instigated by one party to the extent that security can only be taken against that proportion of ownership, not the whole asset, unless the remaining owners agree and execute loan documentation.

> "You can't avoid paying tax by playing dumb! Ignorance is not an excuse!"

15. What about divorce?

Property awarded on divorce through a court property settlement is deemed to have been acquired on the same date as the divorcing spouse acquired it for Capital Gains Tax purposes.

This is why whoever gets the principle place of residence in a split up actually gets more of an advantage down the track than the spouse who gets the investment property or properties, as the investment properties come with a Capital Gains Tax liability when they are eventually sold.

16. What if I build on land I owned pre-CGT?

In this case the building is treated as a separate asset and the proceeds of the sale of land and building are apportioned between the building and the land. The profit from the sale of the land would be Capital Gains Tax exempt and the profit from the sale of the building would have a Capital Gains Tax liability.

17. Contributing capital gains into superannuation

Capital gains can be contributed into superannuation funds and thereby reducing Capital Gains Tax payable.

Superannuation funds over the years have become a great tax shelter and even recent changes to the Superannuation Act have meant more of the benefit payable when you do ultimately retire, will be tax-free. The ability to contribute capital gains into a superannuation fund could mean that ultimately you don't end up paying any tax on the capital gain at all.

The downside is of course that once money is contributed to superannuation it must stay there until you are of legal retirement age,

> "contributing capital gains into a superannuation fund could mean that ultimately you don't end up paying any tax on the capital gain at all"

which at the moment, depending on what year you were born, ranges from 55 to 60. This means your money will no longer be accessible if you are under this age group. On the other hand, if you are nearing or past the 55 to 60 age bracket, realising capital gains and then subsequently contributing capital gains to your superannuation fund can be a highly tax effective strategy.

Superannuation legislation is very complex and I would highly recommend you seek the advice of your accountant as part of any superannuation tax planning decisions.

A quick note on businesses is that not only can business capital gains be rolled over into superannuation; they can also be rolled over into another business. If the business has been owned and run 15 years or more, any capital gain made as a result of the sale of the business will be totally Capital Gains Tax exempt, as it will be treated as a superannuation or a retirement gain.

Chapter 12

The hidden killer - GST!

Unless you have had a lot to do with running a business, GST is probably something you have had little experience with. This certainly is the case for most real estate investors. Consequently, and it is not surprising, they often get themselves into trouble by not understanding their rights and obligations to do with GST. Let's have a look at how GST affects real estate investments.

The Tax Office separates residential rental properties from commercial properties, and treats them differently for GST purposes.

Residential rents

Firstly, residential rents are input taxed and therefore you don't charge GST on the rent. Also, the supplier of the premises (the investor) cannot claim any input tax credits for GST included in the price of supplies acquired for the rental property (e.g. insurance, repairs, agent's commission etc.).

Because residential rents are input taxed and therefore no GST can be claimed on the expenses that relate to that rental income, the rental property is really like having a separate little business. Even if you're a business owner and are registered for GST and you are familiar with lodging BAS forms every three months and charging GST on your invoices and claiming GST on all of your expenses; you will have to segregate the rental income that you're receiving from any of your business income and treat it totally as a separate business.

The income that you receive (that is, the rent), will not have GST paid on it. Therefore, when you pay the electricity bill or the plumber to fix the pipes or anything else, even though they may be charging you GST on their invoices, you can't claim any of it. This is because the expense relates to a piece of residential real estate that is written into the legislation as being input taxed, therefore no GST. However, you can claim the total invoice amount (which includes GST) as a deduction in your tax return at the end of the year.

Since the supply of residential rents is considered to be input taxed (no GST is charged on the rental income), no GST can be claimed on the operating costs such as repairs and maintenance etc. This also means that the sale of a residential property is generally input taxed i.e. no GST is payable on the sale.

However, there are two major exceptions to this general principle:

- the sale of new residential premises

- the sale of commercial residential premises.

What does the Tax Office mean by 'new' residential premises?

The definition of new residential premises becomes very important, because if a property is classified as new the seller must remit one eleventh (1/11) of the sale proceeds to the Tax Office, but on the flip side, they can also claim any GST input credits against the GST collected.

Residential premises are defined as a new residential premises by the Tax Act if they:

- have not previously been sold as residential premises

- have not previously been the subject of a long-term lease

- have sustained substantial renovations to the building

- have been built or contain a building that has been built to replace demolished premises on the same land.

These categories are not mutually exclusive. Provided residential premises satisfy any one of the categories, they will be considered new premises for GST purposes.

The Tax Office has outlined some guidelines for when the sales of properties are considered new residential sales and when they are not. A summary of these are as follows:

1. Residential premises previously sold as commercial residential premises

These may still be sold as new residential premises and therefore may need to have GST collected on sale. For example, where land had only previously been sold with a warehouse constructed on it and the building is converted to residential units, the residential premises would be considered new residential premises. Where a warehouse is converted to residential premises and the resulting residential premises have not been previously sold as residential, or been subject to a long-term lease, sale of the property would count under the GST legislation.

2. Subdivision of apartments into strata titled units

The process of strata titling an apartment block does not, by itself, create new residential premises when the new strata titled units are subsequently sold. The supply of residential units are not new sales of new residential premises, as the land and the building together have previously been sold as residential premises and/or been subject to a long-term lease.

3. New residential premises created through substantial renovations

This is one of the big areas of major confusion for investors. New residential premises may have been created through substantial renovations to the building, and would therefore be subject to GST should the property be sold. However, there is an exception to the substantial renovations rule where the renovations occurred before the 2 December 1998 and the premises were used for residential accommodation before that date. In this case, the sale of the premises is not a taxable supply, and the seller will not need to remit GST on the sale price.

The term substantial renovations as set out in the Tax Act, is defined as follows:-

"Substantial renovations on the building are renovations in which all, or substantially all, of the building is removed or replaced.

However, the renovations need not involve removal or replacement of foundations, external walls, interior supporting walls, floors, roof or staircases."

Whether renovations are substantial or not is to be determined in the light of all the facts and circumstances. For substantial renovations to occur for the purposes of the GST legislation, the renovation needs to satisfy the following criteria before it is necessary to make further inquiry to establish whether the renovations are substantial:-

- The renovation needs to affect the building as a whole, **and**
- The renovations need to result in the removal or replacement of all or substantially all of the building.

Where one of the above criteria is not satisfied, substantial renovations have not occurred and no further inquiry needs to be made. For renovations to be substantial they must directly affect most rooms in the building. If only part of the building is affected by the renovation it would not constitute substantial renovation.

Whether the renovations made to any particular home will constitute substantial renovations is a question of fact to be determined in each case. The ATO is currently developing a draft ruling on this subject.

4. Changes in land size

Where land includes a residential building and is subdivided into two or more lots, and where the land and residential building together have previously been sold or been subject to a long-term lease, even though the land size may have reduced, the sale will not be subject to GST. Subdivision of land will not create new residential premises on its own. However, the supply of vacant land may in fact be a taxable supply in its own right and therefore still be subject to GST upon sale.

5. Removal and relocation of buildings

Where a house has been relocated from one block of land to another, the sale of the old building on the new block of land would be subject to GST, as that house and that block of land have not previously been sold together. If however, the house was relocated from one part of the land to another, and the original house had previously been sold with the previous block of land then the sale would not be subject to GST.

6. When new premises are kept for 5 years and rented out

There is an exception to the normal rules for new premises and that is if the new property is not sold immediately and kept for five years or more as a rental property. Then, the GST legislation for new premises does not apply. Any subsequent sale of the property would not need to have GST remitted on the sale price.

Commercial residential rents

Suppliers of accommodation in commercial residential premises such as hotels and motels that trade etc. are subject to GST, and as such should be treated as commercial, non-residential rentals for GST purposes, even though they do have a residential component.

Guidelines have been set out to assist investors as to what constitutes commercial residential premises.

The establishment must have all of the use characteristics:-

- multiple occupancy;
- commercial intention;
- hiring out to the public (e.g. short-term hire, holiday letting);

- central management;
- services offered (e.g. telephone, laundry etc.).

Commercial non-residential rents

The provision of commercial rental is subject to GST if the provider or owner is registered for GST.

So who has to be registered for GST?

Whether an owner is required to be registered for GST will depend on how much rental income the commercial property earns. If the rental income plus any outgoings paid by the tenant, such as rates and body corporate fees, is $75,000 or more, then the owner is required to be registered for GST. If the total rental income plus the outgoings paid by the tenant are less than $75,000, then the owner has the option to be registered or not.

Commercial Premises

The sale of commercial property by a registered entity will be a taxable supply and subject to GST (whether they are new or used).

There are three methods for calculating GST.

- Normal rules i.e. 10% GST added to value
- Margin Scheme
- GST-free under 'going concern' exemption

REMEMBER:

Stamp Duty is levied on the GST-inclusive value of the commercial property

Tax Secrets of a Real Estate Millionaire

Where possible, sell the property under the GST-free exemption, to avoid Stamp Duty on the GST component.

OMG, I have made a mistake!

Quite often when I'm out talking to people, I find that they have read something somewhere in a newspaper article or something, or tax just hasn't been something that they have wanted to have anything to do with in the past, and quite innocently they have made a mistake. What happens then? What do you do and how do you fix it, or do you just keep your mouth shut and hope that the Tax Office never finds out!

Well I do know a lot of people that have done the latter, but it is not something I recommend.

What should you do, if after reading this book and doing a little bit more research about your own particular situation, you have found that you have actually made a mistake? Maybe you have not charged GST on a new building that you have built. It might have been a house and land which you decided that you might want to use as your principal place of residence, but then you never really lived in it and never ever moved into the building; you decided halfway through that it wasn't what you liked and you wanted to stay where you were, so in the end you just sold it.

The mum and dad who bought the property from you didn't know anything about GST either. They just wanted to live in their new house and of course GST is one of the last things on your mind when you are selling a property. You have just made a nice little profit and all you are thinking about is how you are going to spend the money!

Well, the reality is, in that situation you should have charged GST, or you should've remitted 10% of the sale price to the Tax Office.

So that means for instance, if you bought the land for $150,000 and you spend $250,000 on the house and landscaping and

Tax Secrets of a Real Estate Millionaire

everything else and then after completion, anytime within the next five years, you actually sold the property, you should have charged GST, or you should have remitted to the Tax Office 10% of the sale price.

Now let's just put some numbers to this. Let's say that you sold the property after a year and it had been tenanted for that time. You hadn't quite got around to moving in and

> " Don't just hope that the Tax Office will never find out "

you decided, no, it wasn't what you wanted. So you decided to sell because somebody came along and offered you $500,000 – that's a $100,000 profit; that's worth having!

Now you were very diligent and you knew you had to pay tax on the money and you thought that's all you had to do. That makes sense. You paid your money - what's wrong with that? Well, because it was a new residential property (or a new property of any description for that matter), GST should have been paid when the property was sold as well as paying tax on the $100,000 worth of profit.

Now, if you are reading this and you are thinking 'oh my goodness' and you have started to get cold shivers up your spine and are feeling quite faint because you're in this situation – the best thing to do is to go to your accountant and explain what has happened. He probably didn't even know that you bought and sold a house and land package and declared income on it but maybe not the GST. Because the GST Act actually has a section in it that says, even if you are not registered but could have been registered or should have been registered for GST, you have to pay the GST.

In this case, even though you were not registered for GST, and in fact it hadn't even entered your mind, because the property was sold within the first five years of building the property, then GST is actually payable and you should have been registered for GST.

It basically means that an amendment to your tax return has to be done. The GST will have to be paid. GST will be recalculated and the Tax Office will issue you with a bill for the extra tax that should have been paid. In these circumstances, where you come along and confess and admit that you have made an honest mistake, and you are really sorry, there normally aren't any penalties charged, or if there are, it's a very easy argument for your accountant to lodge an objection and get those penalties quashed.

If on the other hand, you decide not to fess up and the Tax Office finds out about it when they do a tax audit, then I am afraid you are up the proverbial creek without that paddle. Not only will you have to pay the GST that you should have paid, you'll also be hit with **huge** fines, and if the Tax Office decides that wasn't just an innocent mistake, it was actually criminal negligence and tax evasion, then I am afraid there can actually even be a gaol term involved, and believe me, that is not something that you want to do.

Of course, it is not quite as bad as you might initially think, because even though you have to pay GST on the sale price, which if you sold it for $500,000 you would have to pay one eleventh as a GST payment to the tax office = $500,000/11 = $45,454. As a contra to that GST that you have to pay, you can also claim the GST credits on what it has actually cost. So let's go back to the land - it cost $150,000, so if the developer was registered for the GST and was selling you the land as part of a larger development, then for starters there would be GST credits based on that: so 1/11th of $150,000 would be a credit against the GST payable on the sale. This is a credit of $ 13,636.

Then we look at the building costs. Chances are, most of that $250,000 that you have paid to have the home built and landscaped and painted along with all of the other contractors and bits and pieces that you've paid for during the building process, have probably all been registered for the GST as well. That means that you can probably claim 1/11th of that $250,000 as a tax credit = $22,727. So all up, that means your real tax bill is only going to be $9,091 which isn't quite as bad as it first sounded, and certainly better than paying penalties or even facing criminal charges.

Example:

		GST
Property Sale Price	$ 500,000	$ 45,454
Less		
Land Price	$ 150,000	$ 13,636
Building Costs	$ 250,000	$ 22,727
Total GST Credit		$ 36,363
GST now payable		**$ 9,091**

The calculation I have outlined above uses the $1/11^{th}$ rule – in some circumstances it may be more beneficial for you to use the margin scheme for GST. In general terms the margin scheme is more tax efficient if the you are buying the land from a non GST registered seller – you end up paying less tax. If you are buying the land from a registered GST seller, it actually makes no difference.

Chapter 13

Deductions that maximise your profit and cut the cost of tax

By now you must realise that investment in real estate is the most tax effective investment you'll find.

Let's have a look at some of the categories which are tax-deductible when it comes to rental properties.

Accountancy fees

The costs of hiring an accountant to prepare reports associated with the property are fully tax-deductible.

Acquisition and disposal costs

You cannot claim a deduction for the costs of acquiring or disposing of rental property. Examples of expenses of this kind include the purchase cost of the property, conveyancing costs, advertising expenses, and Stamp Duty on the transfer of the property title. However, if you have acquired the property after the 19 September 1985, these costs may form part of a cost base of the property for Capital Gains Tax purposes.

Advertising for tenants

If an agent is managing your property, the expense is normally paid by your managing agent. However, if there are any out-of-pocket expenses to you, the investor, these are fully tax-deductible.

Bank charges

Any fees associated with maintaining the account which receives rent and has expenses paid from it, are fully tax-deductible.

Borrowing expenses

The cost of obtaining finance is mostly considered a capital expense. These costs might include for instance, the legal expenses associated with mortgage documents, Stamp Duty paid on mortgage documents, valuations, surveys, overdraft guarantee fees, search fees etc. The general rule for claiming the cost of borrowing expenses is as follows:-

- if under $100, claim in full in the year of expense
- if over $100, spread the claim over five years
- if the loan is repaid early, any remaining borrowing expenses that have not been already claimed can be claimed in full in the year the loan is repaid.

The costs associated with discharging a mortgage on a property used as security for income producing purposes is also fully deductible.

Body corporate fees

If your property is part of a larger complex, which has common areas, any costs associated with maintaining these common areas by a body corporate is fully tax-deductible.

Body corporate fees and charges may be incurred to cover the cost of day-to-day administration and maintenance, or costs may be applied to a special purpose 'sinking fund'.

If the fees and charges you incur include a contribution to a special purpose sinking fund, you will only be able to claim a deduction for that portion of the fees and charges that relate to the cost of day-to-day administration and maintenance. This is because payments to a special purpose sinking fund are usually to cover the cost of capital improvements or capital repairs. They are therefore not directly tax-deductible.

Cleaning expenses

If the property is rented with cleaning provided, such as those in resort complexes or holiday letting, these expenses are normally deducted by the managing agent prior to you receiving your monthly rental payment and are fully tax-deductible. If cleaning is required after a permanent tenant has vacated your rental property, this fee is also tax-deductible.

Council fees

All fees paid to the local government authority are tax-deductible against the income earned from your investment property.

Deduction for decline in value of depreciating assets

Previously known as depreciation, this has been dealt with in more detail in Chapter 7.

Electricity and gas

In some circumstances, these services are provided to the tenant inclusive in their rental payment, in which case the expense is tax-deductible against the rental income.

Gardening and lawn mowing

These expenses are regular maintenance expenses which can either form part of the rental inclusions when renting a property, or may be periodic expenses when the tenant vacates a property. These expenses are all tax-deductible against the rental income.

In-house audio, video and internet services

Often the provision of these services is an inclusion in the rental of a property. The resultant rental of the property is therefore higher than it normally would have been without these services provided, and thus the expense is fully tax-deductible.

Insurance

Building insurance, contents insurance, landlord insurance and public liability insurance are all tax-deductible against the rental income of the property.

Interest on loans

Interest on money that is borrowed to purchase an income producing property can be claimed as a tax-deduction against the income produced by that property, even if the interest exceeds the rental income, eg. negative gearing

It is important to note that it is the purpose of the funds that determines whether an interest payment will be deductible or not, and this is regardless of what security is used to borrow the funds. The purpose of the funds will usually be determined by the actual use of the funds.

For example, if you buy an investment property and use the equity in another property as security for all or part of the loan, the purpose of the loan was to buy an income producing investment property even though part of the security used to borrow the money could have been your principal place of residence. Conversely, if you borrow money using the equity in an investment property to build a home, swimming pool or add an extension onto your own home, the purpose of the loan would be for private purposes and therefore not tax-deductible, even though an income producing investment property was used as security for the loan.

Lease document expenses

Usually, tenants pay to have leases drawn up. However, if there are any expenses incurred in this process by the investor they will be tax-deductible. These costs might include preparing the lease, registering or stamping the lease documents or having documents amended.

Legal expenses

The Stamp Duty and legal costs of buying a rental property are capital expenses and therefore not tax-deductible. However, if the property has been purchased after the 19 September 1985 and therefore subject to Capital Gains Tax, these non-deductible legal costs may form part of the assets cost base for calculating Capital Gains Tax if sold.

Mortgage discharge expenses

Mortgage discharge expenses are the costs involved in discharging a mortgage other than payments of principle and interest. These costs are tax-deductible in the year that they are incurred to the extent that you took out the mortgage as security for the repayment of money you borrowed to produce assessable income.

Pest control

The regular maintenance and pest control on your rental property is a tax-deduction against the rental income received.

Prepayment expenses

If a prepayment is made on a rental property such as prepayment of insurance or interest on monies borrowed, and the prepayment covers up to 12 months or less and the period ends on or before the 30 June of your income year, you can claim an immediate tax-deduction for the expense.

Property agent's fees and commissions

When you have a property managed by an agent, fees and incidental charges associated with this management service are fully tax-deductible.

Quantity surveyor's fees

A quantity surveyor is a qualified professional who will provide an assessment of the value of your rental property building and improvements and the fixtures and fittings on which you can claim depreciation. This is highly recommended for all rental properties. The fees charged by a quantity surveyor to provide this service are fully tax-deductible.

Repairs and maintenance

The costs of repairing any part of the fixtures and fittings, or the building of a rental property is fully tax-deductible against the rental income. The big question is not whether a repair is tax-deductible, – but whether a repair is actually a repair, or whether it is a capital improvement.

A repair is usually defined as the process of correcting a defective or wornout part, or to return the deteriorated part to its original condition. However, the renewal or replacement of the whole item is not a repair, but is in fact a capital expense and therefore not deductible. Capital expenses of this nature could usually be depreciated under the capital works section of the Tax Act. As a general rule of thumb, unless the material used to make a repair is no longer available or the material used is a more modern equivalent, claims for repairs will not be allowed if a different material is used.

> " timing your repairs is integral to maximising the benefits of your claims "

Carpets for example, are usually replaced when worn, but the replacement is not regarded as a repair, the replaced carpet is considered a capital improvement and is therefore depreciated.

A question I often get asked is, "What if I make a repair to the property after it is no longer income producing?" Well in this case, repairs may still be allowable as a deduction. Even though the property will no longer be available for rent, provided you can show that the repairs are related to the period when the property was used to produce assessable income, it is fine. The Tax Office also takes the view that the premises must have produced assessable income in the year that the expenditure was incurred. This however is just a rule of thumb and not documented in tax law.

The other obvious question when it comes to repairs is, "What about the initial repairs made to a property shortly after its purchase?" Initial repairs made to a property soon after purchase are treated as capital expenses and are therefore added to the cost base for Capital Gains Tax purposes and may be able to be depreciated under the capital works legislation. This applies whether or not the purchase price would have been higher had the property been in better condition. It is better to try and fix any problems associated with your rental property after the property has been rented for a period of time, particularly when it can be shown that the damage could have been caused by tenants after acquisition of the property, as these expenses would then clearly be tax-deductible.

A more comprehensive checklist of deductible expenditure for rental properties can be found in Appendix A.

Timing your repairs

The timing of your repairs is integral to maximising the benefit of any tax-deductions that you may be able to claim. If you're going to be doing a repair to your rental property anyway and you could bring forward that expense into the current financial year, when potentially your other income might be higher; the tax-deduction you would receive for conducting that repair would be worth more to you if incurred in this financial year rather than the next.

When looking at spending money on a rental property, or even a business for that matter, always consider the timing of an expenditure as it may be worth more to you in one particular financial year than another as we explored earlier with our doctor friend in Chapter 6.

Replacement expenses

An immediate deduction is available for depreciating assets costing $300 or less which are used predominately to derive assessable income. These items usually include frequently replaced items or frequently broken items such as crockery, bedding and linen. Also, assets costing less than $1,000 may be written off through the low pool method explained in Chapter 7.

Secretarial and bookkeeping fees

The cost of maintaining adequate records on the rental property is fully tax-deductible.

Security fees

Costs associated with maintaining adequate security on your investment property such as security patrols are fully tax-deductible.

Servicing costs

Regular servicing fees for appliances and fittings are fully tax-deductible.

Stationery, postage, and incidental expenses

These expenses incurred by the landlord on an investment property are fully tax-deductible.

Telephone calls and service rental

The costs associated with preparing taxation returns and recording tax related methods to do with the property are fully tax-deductible.

Travel and car expenses

Travel expenses relating to rent collection, inspection of the property and provision of maintenance of the property are fully tax-deductible, and explained in greater detail in Chapter 10.

Water charges

Water and excess water charges may also be claimed as a tax-deduction against the rental income from the property.

Chapter 14

Finance; making the most of borrowed money

Financing is one of the least understood aspects of investing, yet most people seem to think that they don't need any additional education in this area. The financing game is one that is constantly changing with the advent of new products almost weekly, as well as changes in interest rates, fees, charges and even hidden charges.

Taxpayers have to be exceptionally careful as to how their loans are structured and how their payments and money flows are made, as this has a dramatic effect on whether the payment of interest on a loan is tax-deductible or not.

Tax Secrets of a Real Estate Millionaire

Purpose of the funds test

The golden rule when it comes to financing and tax is:

What is the purpose of the loan?

If you can argue your case to the Tax Office that the purpose of the loan, that is, the application of the funds, was for investment purposes, then the interest on that loan will be tax-deductible against any income that investment yields.

So many times I have people come to me with stories about how they are currently living in their principal place of residence, but it's either too small, too big, too this or too that, and they want to move out and purchase another principal place of residence.

> *"regardless of where the money is secured, the tax-deductibility test relies solely on the purpose of the funds"*

The usual question I get is, "We really want to keep our current home as an investment property when we move out of it and purchase our new principal place of residence - do you think that's a good idea?"

Well of course, if they can afford it, I think it's a good idea, but when I start to question them about how they are structuring their finances, the usual response I get is, "Well, the bank said it was okay for us to borrow the money for the new property and because our current principal place of residence will be an investment property we will be able to save on our taxes won't we?" Now my answer to that of course is a big fat, "No".

You see, the taxpayer is probably borrowing the money based on the security of both properties to buy their new principal place of residence. Therefore, the purpose of the funds is to buy a principal place of residence, not an investment property. Regardless of where the money is secured the tax deductibility test relies solely on the purpose of the funds. If the purpose of the funds is to buy another investment property, then no problem, but if the purpose of the funds is to buy their new principal place of residence irrespective of security, the Tax Office will not allow the interest as a tax-deduction.

One little legal loophole

If the mortgage was relatively low on the current principal place of residence - it may be worthwhile transferring or selling the property to a trust. This would be treated as a sale but of course no Capital Gains Tax would be payable because the property was a principal place of residence. Stamp Duty, on the other hand, would be payable.

However, when you analyse the costs of paying Stamp Duty versus the benefit of having the interest on a much greater amount tax-deductible, in the long term the client might be better to wear a small short-term negative for a greater long-term deductibility.

Let me work you through an example to show you what I'm talking about:-

John and Edith have a nice 3 bedroom house that they have paid off over the years. As the family has grown, they are finding that the house is a little bit small. Two of their three teenage children had shared a bedroom as they were growing up,

" it may be worthwhile transferring or selling the property to a trust"

but now that they are older, they would like their own rooms as well as a little bit of a separate area so that they can have their friends over, and John and Edith can still have their own private space.

Tax Secrets of a Real Estate Millionaire

Now, their house has been valued at $500,000 and the mortgage is entirely paid off, so they are in a good position to borrow some money from the bank to purchase the new 4 bedroom house with a pool and entertainment area that they have fallen in love with. John and Edith have decided that rather than sell their existing home, that they would like to keep it as an investment property, as it is in a good area which has great growth potential, and they could rent it out to help make the payments on their new home.

The bank has agreed to loan them the entire $650,000 to purchase their new home using their existing principal place of residence as security to cover the deposit and costs of this new home.

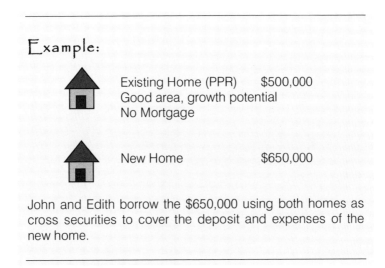

Example:

Existing Home (PPR) $500,000
Good area, growth potential
No Mortgage

New Home $650,000

John and Edith borrow the $650,000 using both homes as cross securities to cover the deposit and expenses of the new home.

Not the best strategy!

Now, as you can see, this is easy enough to do, but this is not a strategy that I would encourage for the following reasons:-

Firstly, because John and Edith have borrowed the money to purchase a new principal place of residence, even though they have secured the loan on what will be an investment property, and they will be producing income by renting out their previous home, none of their interest or associated mortgage fees will be tax-deductible. This is because they have borrowed the money to purchase their **new** principal place of residence. Had they bought an investment property with the borrowed money all these same expenses would have been fully tax-deductible. But of course, that is not what they wanted, they wanted a new home.

Secondly, because the existing home has been used as security to make their new principal place of residence purchase, they have now put themselves at the mercy of the bank or financial institution, next time they want to go off and buy a property. This is called cross-securitisation. At first glance, cross-securitisation sounds fine, and from a bank's perspective it is also fine, but it is something that I would strongly suggest that you try to avoid.

What the bank is doing, is tying up all of John and Edith's available equity so that John and Edith have to go back to the same bank next time they want to borrow money for anything – whether that is to extend the house, put in a new kitchen, buy another investment property or even a portfolio of shares. It is a great trick from the bank's perspective to retain clients, but it is cumbersome, and can be downright dangerous from John and Edith's perspective.

Let me share with you a couple of stories from clients of mine, just to show you how important non cross-securitisation really is.

One of my clients ran service stations in central Queensland. He had been with the one bank for over 30 years, doing all his lending and banking with that same bank. He knew the local bank manager personally and had never missed a payment, nor were his repayments ever late. One day, some little dweeb in head office at the bank that he had used for the last 30 years, decided it was bank policy that they no longer wanted to have exposure in service station roadhouses in regional areas. So, after 30 years of good behaviour and loyalty to his bank, he was given 30 days notice to refinance elsewhere!

What was worse, is that he had all his loans tied up with this one bank - his rural property, commercial property, residential home and business loans, were all financed through this bank, and consequently cross-securitised.

> "Always separate your principal place of residence away from any other lending you may have"

Therefore, when his loans were called in, **all** of his loans were called in - not just the loans which affected the service station.

Now as any business person knows, if you are put in a situation where you have to refinance in 30 days, you are not always market ready. You may not have your tax returns done for the previous year, for instance, or even have your bookkeeping ready to present to prospective lenders. Well, this client was no different.

He was unable to refinance the loans within the 30 day period, and as a result, the bank automatically put him on default interest rates which at the time were 13.75%. Now, at that rate, my client did start to default on his repayments.

When you are on default interest rates with one bank, it is nigh on impossible to refinance with another bank, regardless of your previous 30 years of good behaviour. Any new bank will shy away simply because they are suspicious of why you are now on the default interest rates, and as a consequence, my client, who was in his late 50's, lost everything he owned; everything he had worked over 30 years to accumulate.

The stress subsequently gave him a heart attack and it was only through some really good negotiation, and a lot of luck that we were able to save him from going bankrupt entirely, and that his daughter was able to purchase the home where they lived so that her parents would not be left completely homeless.

You see, in most mortgage loan documents, there is a clause called the 'all monies clause', which stipulates that if there is ever a default or a reason to recall on any one loan with that particular bank, all loans with that bank can be called in. Normally speaking, the easiest place for the bank to get their money is from your principal place of residence. So guess which property they're going to sell up first?

This is precisely the reason that I am very much opposed to cross-securitisation, and why I always advocate, at the very minimum, to keep your principal place of residence home loan with a separate bank or financial institution.

The story I have just outlined is not an uncommon incident. I have seen it happen in the building industry where there is a downturn in the property market and builders and developers become the target.

Sometimes, even investors get caught up in head office bank policy, and have their loans called in simply because of media-hype and uneasiness about a particular industry. I've seen it happen in the dairy industry when milk vending was deregulated. A friend of a friend who was a milk vendor on the Gold Coast, for no apparent reason other than because of his occupation, had all of his loans called in by one particular bank, because they felt uneasy about the milk industry.

I also remember years ago, talking to a lady who was head of the Dairy Farmer's Association in South Australia, and she was telling me about dairy farms in South Australia that had been repossessed by the banks because they no longer wanted exposure to the milk industry whilst it was in a state of flux, post-deregulation. Farms that had been in families for generations were being repossessed by the banks.

So one of my golden rules is:-

Always separate your principal place of residence away from any other lending you may have.

Sometimes, through practicality you may have two or three loans with the one bank, but your home will still be with a separate bank. As you start to become a seasoned investor you will become a first class client to the commercial manager with many banks.

So, what should John and Edith have done?

Well, it is a little complicated, but in the long term it would have saved John and Edith thousands of dollars in tax.

Rather than borrowing the money for their new house from the bank, John and Edith could sell their existing home to a trust. The trust pays John and Edith $500,000, 95% ($475,000) of which has been borrowed from the bank to purchase the house.

The remaining 5% ($25,000) is loaned back to the trust by John and Edith. As it has been John and Edith's principal place of residence, they do not have to pay Capital Gains Tax, but the trust will have to pay Stamp Duty - John and Edith would probably have to lend the trust the money for this as well.

So now John and Edith have $475,000 to put down as a deposit on their new home. They are still $175,000 short to buy their $650,000 home, so they would have to borrow that amount from the bank to make up the difference.

This is how this structure would look:

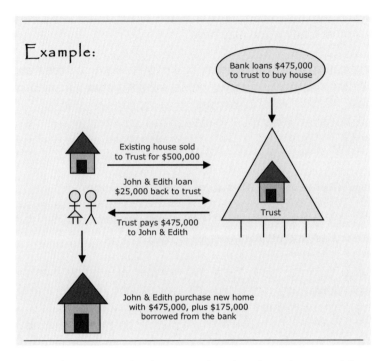

Now the interest on the $175,000 that they have borrowed from the bank personally to purchase their new home is not tax-deductible, but the interest on the $475,000 borrowed through the trust to purchase the home from John and Edith, which will now be rented out, can be claimed against the income generated from that property.

Although in the first year there will be no great benefit to John and Edith as they will have had to pay Stamp Duty, after the second year and every year thereafter, there will be considerable tax savings from claiming the interest on the borrowed money which they would not have been able to claim had they borrowed the money to purchase their new principal place of residence.

This is how the numbers would look:

Example:

Loan	$ 475,000
Tax-Deductible Interest @ 7.5%	$ 35,625
Tax Saved (estimated @ 30%)	$ 10,687
Cost of Stamp Duty (est.)	$ 15,000

After approximately 1½ years the cost of the Stamp Duty will have been made up by the tax saved, so every year after that, that they continue to own the property, they will be $10,687 ahead.

So you see, by simply changing the method in which you purchase your new principal place of residence, you have the ability to save money that you would have had to pay in tax by doing something that you were going to do anyway, in this case, purchase your new home.

Converting bad debt to good debt

There is often talk about 'good debt' and 'bad debt', but there is also often some confusion over what 'good debt' and 'bad debt' actually is. The distinction between good debt and bad debt is as follows:-

Bad debt can be categorised as consumer debt and non-deductible debt. Usually, this is debt that has been incurred to buy consumable items before you have the money available, (saved or earned) to pay loans for them, e.g. furniture and store card debt, car loans (if not used for business or income producing

> *"good debt interest is tax-deductible... bad debt interest is not"*

purposes), holiday loans, credit card debt and to a lesser extent, your personal home loan.

Good debt on the other hand, is debt that has been incurred for the purpose of making more income, i.e. for income producing purposes. For example, investment property loans, share investment loans or a business loan (provided it is a profitable business).

Normally, the good debt interest is tax-deductible... bad debt interest is not.

The real trick is to convert bad debt to good debt, and thereby have your interest payments tax-deductible.

Smart money flow

Smart money flow is making any income that you earn work for you from the moment you receive it, by applying it to debt that you will receive the least tax advantage from, and to reduce that debt as quickly as possible.

Smart money flow tips:

1. Have all your money deposited into a private line-of-credit, offset or redraw split loan facility.

2. Structure the loan so that interest is calculated on a daily balance.

3. Take advantage of 55 day interest free periods on credit cards.

4. Pay off credit cards on or before due date – this can be set up so that it is done automatically.

5. Have a second credit card that is linked to your investment account so any expenses are already

> 6. Pay repayments weekly or fortnightly on personal accounts and monthly on your investment account.

By utilising 'smart money flow', anyone, including John and Edith have the possibility of reducing their $175,000 loan much quicker than traditional principal and interest never-never plans.

When the realisation of just how effective this money flow capacity really was, there were some organisations that were charging $4,000-$10,000 to set up these types of loan facilities for individuals. In fact, there are still a few stragglers out there in the marketplace that provide some fancy computer programs and budgeting advice, and charge similar amounts for the setting up of loan facilities that maximise cash flow to the borrower's advantage.

When you utilise the systems of smart money flow, what you are predominantly trying to do, is reduce the debt on your personal account as fast as you can. You need to get all your money flowing, and any income, whether it be wages or rental income or any other source of income that you have, offsetting the balance on your personal loan account.

To get the most out of your money flow, you can get your rents paid into your personal account weekly, as well as your wages and any other accessible income, while just paying the interest on your investment account monthly. What this will achieve is that over the duration of the month, because you are making payments weekly, and interest is calculated daily, it will reduce the balance on your personal account quite quickly. The additional benefit is that because you are reducing the debt quickly on your personal account, where the interest payments are not tax-deductible, while just maintaining the minimum payments on your investment account, it is also reducing the amount of non tax-deductible interest that you would have had to pay over the duration of the loan.

Tax Secrets of a Real Estate Millionaire

Loan splitting

Effectively a split loan is two separate loan accounts that have a seemingly invisible accounting line between the loans. There are two ways in which this facility is usually set up. Some banks set it up within the one structure and create sub-accounts, while some banks do require you to set up two separate accounts.

A split loan facility is extremely important when it comes to managing your loans, and is primarily to keep your investment or business debt, i.e. your tax-deductible debt, clearly separated from your personal debt, i.e. principal place of residence, car, credit cards, etc.

So, a split loan, by its invisible line or separation, defines exactly what portion of the loan is for personal use and what portion is for business use. It clearly categorises, for tax purposes,

> " a split loan defines exactly what portion of the loan is for personal use or for business use "

what interest can be claimed. If the purpose of the loan is not defined, then it is left to your accountant to try to work out what portion of the payments is in fact deductible, often resulting in you, the tax payer, paying much more tax than need be, simply because you are unable to make that distinction.

Splits or loan limits can be readjusted at anytime so that more or less can be drawn for investment or for personal use and can be done quite easily, as you are not actually asking for more money - you are just altering the split.

Let's catch up with John and Edith again. Remember they had bought a new principal place of residence worth $650,000 with a private loan of $175,000 against it.

John and Edith bought their house for $650,000 which meant that their maximum lending capacity would be up to 80% by way of a line-of-credit or redraw facility, which they could use to pay off their $175,000 loan, and use the excess to buy another investment property. In this instance, their lending capacity would be $520,000.

From this $520,000, they would split the loan at $200,000 for personal purposes. This would cover the $175,000 personal home loan and give them a 'buffer' of $25,000 as back up funds to draw on in the case of an emergency.

If John was ill or if his car broke down, or even if he and Edith had a family emergency that required them to travel at short notice, they would have funds they could access quickly without stretching their finances unreasonably, and it would be enough to cover any repayments in the short term.

A buffer is for protection for anything unforseen that may arise.

In the instance of an investment property, they would need a buffer also. They might not be insured for loss of rental when a tenant leaves, or they may have long-term vacancies, or they may need to make some urgent repairs. It gives the borrower time to work out something or deal with the issues, without putting pressure on their day to day cash flow.

So, John and Edith's buffer is $25,000 for their personal loan and $20,000 for their investment loan, which leaves them $300,000 with which to purchase a new investment property.

The line-of-credit on John and Edith's home is split as follows:

Tax Secrets of a Real Estate Millionaire

Example:

Principal Place of Residence value	$ 650,000
Line-of-credit / redraw facility (80% of value)	$ 520,000
Split 1 – Personal ($175,000 loan + buffer $25,000) *Interest payments are not tax-deductible*	$ 200,000
Split 2 – Investment ($300,000 available + buffer $20,000) *Interest payments are tax-deductible*	$ 320,000

Now, if John and Edith had set up their line-of-credit or redraw facility without any distinction between business and personal, then it would be extremely hard for their accountant to identify what interest and expenses were personal and what were for the purpose of investment. Any interest payments would be distributed evenly between the two, rather than specifically towards the account for which it was intended, resulting in possible waste of tax deductibility.

At this point you might ask, "What happens if they receive a lump sum, if, for instance, they sold their car?" The best thing to do would be to deposit the money against their private debt. If they sold the car and put the money towards their line-of-credit and they didn't have a split facility, then they would be paying down both debts, whereas if they did have a split loan, they could choose to just pay down their personal loan as the car was for private use.

Now they could also adjust the proportions of the split on their loan. If they received $10,000 for their car and apply that money to their personal split, they can now reduce that proportion by $10,000 which will give them $10,000 more that can be spent on investments.

The loan splits would now be:

Example:

Split 1 – Personal	$ 190,000
($165,000 loan + Buffer $25,000)	
Split 2 – Investment	$ 330,000
($310,000 available + Buffer $20,000)	
Total Line-of-credit	**$ 520,000**

If John and Edith's granny died and left them $50,000, and they needed to 'park' this money somewhere for a short period of time while they decided what to do with it, they would be best off to apply it to their personal debt.

Again, they could alter the split to reduce the limit on their personal loan, and increase the limit on their investment loan in turn changing the purpose of the funds to suit investing in the future.

The other alternative is to park the money in an offset account.

Offset accounts

An offset account is a savings account that has the ability to offset the interest, dollar for dollar, that is drawn on your loan account. So if you have a savings account that is linked to your personal debts, every dollar that you have sitting in that account will reduce the interest that you have in your loan account as if that same amount was applied to that loan. Effectively, it is a direct saving and you are earning between 5% - 6.5% (depending on your interest rate) on your money and even better. This is a savings benefit that you are getting TAX-FREE.

Tax Secrets of a Real Estate Millionaire

The purpose of the funds

While John and Edith loved the home that they had bought and lived in for a number of years, circumstances had changed. John had got a new job on the other side of town and the kids had grown up and were, one by one, leaving home. Over the years they had determined exactly what sort of home they would next like to live in. So they made the decision to sell their home and build their dream home closer to John's new job.

> Ask yourself first, "What is the future purpose of the funds?"

From the sale of their home, John and Edith had $200,000 which they wanted to put towards the new home that they were building but they needed to park it somewhere for the short term while they were getting organised.

Their first inclination was to put the money into the line-of-credit that they had on one of their investment properties. By doing this, they would have altered the nature of the funds to their disadvantage. By paying the money off their investment account, and then later redrawing it to build their new home, they would be converting their investment loan into a private loan, because the purpose of the funds was personal purposes rather than investment purposes, and the interest payments would then no longer be tax-deductible.

So what should John and Edith be doing with these funds?

The best thing to do is to park the money in an offset account. This way, the money can sit in an account that remains external to their loan. The loan balance remains the same but the interest actually gets reduced – effectively it is the same as paying down the loan. When it comes to building their new house in the future and reutilising the money, the nature of the funds has not altered within the account. They are getting the best of both worlds as they have the ability to reduce the interest for the time that they have the money in their hands, but they don't have to reduce their loan or change the nature of their loan in an adverse way.

When you receive any lump sums of money that you want to utilise in the short term, the question you need to ask yourself is, "What is the future use of the money?"

The Golden Rule:
If the future use is going to be for investment, then it is fine to pay off the personal or investment debt as its future use is going to be to redraw the funds as investment debt. However, if future use of that money is going to be for personal purposes, then do not use this money to pay off investment debt, use an offset account that is going to offset interest on your personal debt.

Chapter 15

Family arrangements, Investing with children

Quite often, parents lend a helping hand financially with their children's first investment property or home. Although there are many ways in which you could go about this, care needs to be taken with shared equity ownership, the First Home Owner's Grant and beneficial interests through trust structures.

Shared equity ownership

When it comes to shared equity ownership, parents need to decide whether they are giving their child a loan or they are actually buying a property with their child. Both have very different ramifications on profit, structure, tax and even the First Home Owner's Grant.

Firstly, let's talk about the First Home Owner's Grant.

First Home Owner's Grant

The Australian Government introduced the current First Home Owner's Grant scheme on the 1 July 2000 to offset the effect of GST on home ownership.

Clearly, if a child is entitled to the First Home Owner's Grant, it would be a shame to compromise their eligibility for the grant by buying a jointly owned home first off.

Parents would be better to lend their child the deposit to purchase the property, and additional funds if required for renovations, purchase costs etc., and have their child repay that loan, rather than take an equity position in the property, as this would negate their eligibility for the First Home Owner's Grant.

If the parent was looking to share in the profits that the child may make from, for instance, a renovation on the property, or growth arising from the property that the parent has helped them buy, then this would have to be done purely as a private arrangement. The child would be the legal owner of the property, and as such, any entitlements to gains from the sale of the property at any point in time in the future would belong to the child. Similarly, because the property would be the child's principal place of residence, any gain arising from the sale of the property would be Capital Gains Tax exempt.

I have known parents to charge their child for labour, management fees and interest on the loan equivalent to their share from the sale of the property, but I must stress, that this must purely be a private arrangement for the child to still be eligible for concessional Stamp Duty and the Capital Gains Tax exemption for a principal place of residence. Also, any amount received by the parent from the child for such expenses would of course be treated as income in the parent's name. No Capital Gains Tax exceptions would be able to be applied as their payment is effectively an income payment. Whilst the income would be tax-free to the child, the parents' share or any monies paid to them would be Income Tax assessable in their tax returns.

Furthermore, if the parent was structured correctly and utilising structures such as a 'bucket company' to store tax paid money, the parent could actually lend the child the money from their bucket company. The bucket company would then in turn receive interest payments back from the child periodically or as a lump sum 'balloon' payment when the child ultimately refinances or realises the gain on the property through sale. These payments would be Income Tax accessible to the bucket company which of course would be taxed at a maximum rate of 30 cents in the dollar.

Another way which parents look to help their child out is by purchasing a property through a family discretionary trust structure where the child is a beneficiary of the trust. In this type of arrangement, the child is not the legal owner of the property, and therefore would not be entitled to concessional Stamp Duty or the First Home Owner's Grant, and similarly, Capital Gains Tax would have to be paid on the profit on sale of the property.

Using this style of trust structure would be just like any other property from a parents' perspective, except they would be sharing the profits with their child. It is often a good opportunity to teach their child the ropes in a protected environment and potentially give the child a kick start when they buy their first principal place of residence in their own name, after the initial trust structure purchase.

Tax Secrets of a Real Estate Millionaire

Who can apply for the first home owner's grant?

The **First Home Owner's Grant**[3] is a lump sum payment of $7,000 with additional Mortgage Duty and Transfer Duty concessions depending on the state that you live in. The grant has no tax benefit initially other than the reduction of these duties at the time of purchase, as the house must be the grant applicant's principal place of residence for at least 6 months, and must be resided in for this period of time within the first 12 months of purchasing.

Applicant eligibility is as follows:
- Must be at least 18 years of age on the date of the transaction.
- Only one grant/application is payable per transaction.
- All persons that will have an interest as purchaser or owner in the home must complete an application form.
- Applications must be lodged within one year after the purchase/transaction of the home.

The eligibility criteria are:
- You must have a construction or purchase contract in place for your first home made on or after 1 July 2000; and
- You must reside in the home relating to your grant application as a principal place of residence for at least six months within one year of the completion of the transaction.

Applicant's obligations:
- To provide thorough and correct information for purpose of assessing eligibility.

---

[3] As stated at time of printing on *http://www.firsthome.gov.au*

- Notify the Commissioner if you do not fulfil the requirements with regards to residence or the application criteria.
- To repay the grant where the conditions of the grant are not met.

A home for the purpose of a grant is defined as:
- A fixed building that is a suitable place of residence. This includes houses, flats, units, townhouses and kit homes.
- The home must be located in the state in which you are applying for the grant.
- The home must be established or under contract to be built.

Renting your way through uni

So, your children are growing up and one by one they are off to university. With that often comes the need for accommodation close to their university, as well as a long list of expenses that go hand-in-hand with studying; school fees, text books and general living expenses. It can be a very expensive time.

There are many ways in which these situations can be turned to your advantage, to not only provide a home for your child while they are living away from home studying, but also to help offset some of the other expenses.

For example, I had a client whose son needed to move to Brisbane to be close to his university. He decided to purchase a home in Brisbane for $265,000. He converted the 5 bedroom house into a 7 bedroom house, by dividing some of the larger living spaces into the extra bedrooms. His son then leased the house from his father, equal to the total of the rates, insurance and interest on the mortgage, therefore making the property cashflow neutral. Then his son subleased the 6 extra rooms to other tenants. By subleasing the 6 rooms at $100 each, the son was able to create a passive income of $600 per week that went towards his university fees.

There were two gains in this instance. The father got the capital gain on the property and he was able to see his son through university at no additional cost to him. The only thing that you do need to remember is that the son's income from the rent is assessable and that when making the renovations, the house does need to comply with council regulations, and have the relevant insurances.

Investing income for children

Owning shares or having money invested in children's names, or even having children share in profits from properties held in trust structures, becomes very interesting when the children are under 18 years of age.

This type of income is called 'unearned income' to the child and is taxed differently from if the child was old enough to hold down a part time job delivering papers, or work at a fast food chain or do some administration work or filing for you at home, and actually earn an income.

Unearned income has different thresholds for minors. Appendix G shows the eligible income thresholds for minors, and as you can see any income earned over and above $416 is taxed at the exceptionally high rate of 66%. This then falls back to a 45% level over $1307.

I had a young couple come and ask me how old their child had to be to receive a distribution from their trust as they had a newborn who was born in June, close to the end of the financial year. Basically, as long as the child is born on or before the 30 June, the end of the financial year, the child is eligible to receive a distribution of $416, effectively tax-free.

Tax Secrets of a Real Estate Millionaire

There are exceptions to the unearned income rules such as when the child commences employment, or if they have some sort of disability and are therefore entitled to a pension or allowance for this disability, or if the child receives income distributions from a testamentary trust (i.e. a trust set up to care for minor children as a result of a Will). In these instances, they would be considered 'excepted persons' and normal tax rates would apply to them.

There is also the occasion where the 'type' of income of the child is excepted, for instance, employment income, income from deceased estates or their own businesses or investments deriving from these excepted incomes. Again, normal tax rates would apply.

See our table in Appendix G for Tax Rates for Non-excepted Minors.

Children's earned income

As I have mentioned, there is a distinct difference between unearned income and earned income with children. I now want to focus on earned income and when I say children what I am really talking about is minors under the age of 18, but children old enough to actually perform job-worthy duties for an employer.

These days, children are able to join the workforce with employers such as retail outlets, delivery organisations and fast-food outlets from the age of 13 or 14. Therefore, it is not inconceivable that these children could have paid employment within your structure or organisation/business for a similar paid wage.

My daughter, Samantha, has been doing my filing, entering expenses, cash receipts and bank and credit card statements, into my accounting system since she was 10. This is a job I would normally pay someone else to do if she was not performing the tasks. Consequently, paying her to do the job is saving my company money, and fulfilling normal operational activities within the company.

To pay her a wage for doing this work, she must have a Tax File Number, be registered to receive superannuation contributions and lodge a tax return at the end of the financial year. As a responsible director of an operational company, I am obligated to pay her award wages for the hours actually worked.

This is a really great way of making your kids work-ready, responsible with money, and know the value of the dollar. However, beyond that, it is also a responsible way of dealing with the profits in your structure. Even though Samantha is under the age of 18, because she is earning the income as opposed to just receiving distributions from a trust, she is entitled to be taxed as an adult and therefore receives the first $18,200 of her Income Tax-free.

Let's just apply a little bit of lateral thinking here. If Samantha is earning a fair wage from the hours she is working, she could also be held responsible to pay for some of the expenses which relate to her, and are clearly of a private nature for which I would otherwise be responsible. What I'm talking about is her clothes, shoes, school fees, etc., that I would normally have to pay for from my after-tax monies. Provided she earns sufficient income to cover these expenses, effectively I would be getting a tax-deduction via her employment in which she performs a useful task for the company, and for her school fees which I would otherwise have to pay for from after-tax monies.

In normal circumstances I would say 12 is a little bit young to handle such responsibility, but you don't know my daughter!

In most circumstances, strategies such as this are normally implemented at an age which any other employer would be happy to take on the child under normal employment conditions. That age is normally about 13½ to 14½ years of age.

This is not a strategy to be abused, and the child must actually be performing the tasks they are being paid to perform, and they must be paid according to regular award wages for juniors performing such tasks.

Divorce

Divorce is always tricky. However, as a general rule, when tax has to be paid from a property venture, regardless of whether it is income arising from the rental of a property or capital gain arising from the sale of a property, the person who acquires the property out of the divorce settlement will be the one responsible for the Income Tax liability. If for instance, the property was jointly owned, the couple go through divorce and let's say the husband was awarded the property in the property settlement, he would have been deemed to have acquired the property in his own right at the same time as he and his spouse did, when the property was originally purchased.

If divorce took place part way through a sub-division or development or any kind of manufactured growth structure, it would be the party who ended up with the property out of the divorce settlement who would be responsible for the Income Tax and GST liabilities.

Of course, if the property was owned through a structure, divorce may have little Income Tax implication on the end result. For example, if a trust structure owned a sub-division, a piece of real estate or development property, when the divorce took place, the ultimate responsibility and ownership of the property and beneficial ownership would rest with the party that was awarded the shares in any trustee company. Any beneficial ownership of the property out of the property settlement would be the responsibility of the beneficial owner.

Whilst divorce and Family Law Courts see through all structures, the Income Tax liability goes with the Family Law Court property distribution to the party who is awarded the property. Even if the property is held through trust structures, whilst the tax may not necessarily have to be paid by the individual if the property was owned in a trust structure, if the party was granted the property through the Family Law Court property settlement, the divorcing party could still have profits distributed to other structures and bucket companies, just like they would have done prior to divorce.

Chapter 16

Succession planning, what happens if you inherit?

Succession planning is a nice term for talking about a topic no one likes to talk about: what happens when you die?

Even though it might be a taboo topic at barbecues and social outings, it is something that needs to be taken into account as part of an overall investment strategy.

So what is succession planning? It is the process of dealing with the transfer of assets in the event of death, from one generation to the next.

The legal document required to take account of this transference of assets is commonly known as the legal Will.

So what is a Will?

A Will is a legally enforceable declaration directing the disposal of a person's property upon their death. If you die without a Will, or with an invalid Will, according to the law you will be considered to have died 'intestate' and your estate will be divided up according to the legislation in the state or territory in which you lived by the Public Trustee's Office.

A Will is therefore an extremely important document if you want to exercise your legal rights of directing to whom, and in what manner, your assets should be distributed upon your death, and of appointing someone to look after your affairs. To be valid, a Will must be in writing, either hand-written, typed or a combination of both and must be signed by the person making the Will in the presence of two independent witnesses and to be really pedantic to prove all parties were present at the same time, the Will should also be signed with the same pen by all parties.

> "It is important to regularly review your will. It is recommended that this is done every two to three years or whenever a significant change occurs in your family circumstances, assets or relevant taxation laws"

Making out a Will is not an overly expensive exercise, but just as we have outlined in previous chapters, the more knowledge you have on a particular subject, the better the chances are that you will make the right decisions. This also holds true when making out your Will.

Firstly, let's look at why you need a Will in the first place and how a well thought out estate plan can help minimise problems in the future.

Estate planning has two main aims:

1. To try to avoid the likelihood of any next-of-kin suffering financially; and

2. To minimise the risk of family squabbles about who gets what.

Estate planning was initially used when there were death and estate duties, and even though these no longer exist in Australia, there are other taxes, such as Capital Gains Tax, that make estate planning just as worthwhile now.

An estate plan should:

- Be administratively simple to operate;

- Be relatively inexpensive to maintain;

- Balance life-time enjoyment of assets/income with preserving assets for family after death; and

- Be regularly reviewed

Early planning, good advice and the proper assembly of important documents will all ensure that your estate is handled as easily as possible.

Whilst every situation is different when it comes to preparing an individual Will, the following issues may be relevant and therefore assist in preparing a thorough estate plan:-

- A good estate plan should take into account both your personal and financial situation. For example, some families have minor children who will need to be cared for whilst others may own and operate a business that needs consideration.

- All assets of any value should be considered when developing an estate plan, including real estate, business and farm interests, investments, retirement plans, life insurance proceeds, personal property, art or other collections, cash and personal effects.

- Take into consideration the fair market value of your assets, how you own them legally, their growth potential, their liquidity, and what assets should be passed to specific individuals.

Remember, your estate plan should provide you with the comfort of knowing that your wishes will be carried out should anything happen to you in the future. This benefits not only you, but also your family members, who otherwise may face the burden of making choices for you without your input and under stress or mourning.

As with all of your asset protection measures, it is important to regularly review your Will. It is recommended that this is done every two to three years or whenever a significant change occurs in your family circumstances, assets or relevant taxation laws.

In particular, you should review your Will if:

- You change your name, or any person named in the Will changes their name;

- An executor dies or becomes unwilling to act as executor or becomes unsuitable due to age, ill health or any other reason;

- A beneficiary named in your Will dies;

- You have specifically left any property which you have subsequently sold, given away, put into trust or into a partnership which changes its character. This applies particularly to specifically bequeathed shares in a company which restructures its share capital;

- You marry or divorce or if you have children (including adopted or fostered children). A Will automatically becomes invalid if you marry, unless the Will is said to have been made in contemplation of your marriage;

- You enter into, or end, a de-facto relationship.

Enduring Power of Attorney

Just as it is important to carefully consider and plan your Will, it is equally important to set up an Enduring Power of Attorney. This is basically a legal instrument authorising another person to act as your attorney or agent in the event of your incapacity, due to illness or accident.

As this person has the power to make personal and/or financial decisions on your behalf, it goes without saying that they should be extremely trustworthy.

Powers of Attorney have three main purposes:

- If you are travelling or otherwise incapacitated, they can carry out financial transactions on your behalf;

- You can authorise this person to make personal decisions while you are unable to manage your affairs, such as if you were incapacitated like being in a coma or affected by a stroke etc.;

- They can also make provisions for a power to consent to medical treatment and medical donations.

Tax Secrets of a Real Estate Millionaire

The whole concept of having a Power of Attorney in place in the event of something happening which may render you incapacitated, is very close to my heart. My father was very much of the old school and believed all assets should be held in the man's name. He dealt with all financial matters of the family and owned all the assets, bank accounts etc in his name. Now you know why I'm such a control freak when it comes to the finances!

> *"make sure all aspects of your estate and the consequences of your decision have been considered"*

Dad was in the middle of selling one property in order to buy another when he had a stroke which rendered him unable to speak or communicate in any fashion. The legal turmoil which followed in the midst of obvious family stress was that legal documentation had to be drawn up and signed by Mum and all the seven children in my family, giving Mum the right to access the family finances and deal with the legal obligations and increasing penalties associated with defaulting on the sale and purchase of the property. Mum even had trouble reregistering the car since it was registered in his name.

The whole exercise cost the family several thousands of dollars, unnecessarily. Had Dad simply had a one page Power of Attorney in place enabling Mum to take over his affairs whilst incapacitated, none of this would ever have happened.

> *"advance planning will ensure that the trustee has the discretion to distribute assets accordingly"*

What renders a Will invalid?

There may be any number of reasons why a Will could be rendered invalid. It may be thought that the Will presented was not in fact the 'last' Will of the deceased, or it may be thought that the deceased lacked the mental capacity to make the Will or that they might not have understood the Will. It may also be thought that they were pressured into changing the Will or even worse, that it has fraudulently been changed by someone else. Alternatively, there is also the event in which the deceased may not have adequately provided for spouses or children that have been left behind and that they may suffer hardship as a result of the deceased's wishes and therefore they contest the Will for reallocation of the deceased's estate.

They are all valid reasons which can result in the Will being rendered invalid, and will have the same consequences as that of a person who died intestate. Probably the most important factor when drafting a Will is that it is signed by two independent witnesses and ensuring that all aspects of your estate and consequences of your decision have been considered. I believe getting professional help is a must – doing it yourself is asking for trouble.

Testamentary trusts

A **testamentary trust** is a real tax vehicle trust which effectively forms part of your Will and has specific tax implications for the beneficiaries of the trust, in particular minors, i.e. dependants under the age of 18.

The tax benefits of this type of structure are extremely important, but the asset protection benefits of setting up a testamentary trust are also relevant.

Basically, setting up a testamentary trust means that unless assets have been specifically allocated to a particular beneficiary, the assets of a testamentary trust do not form part of the estate of the person controlling the trust nor of any beneficiaries.

A testamentary trust can also be of benefit to parents of young children. The assurance that their children will be looked after for living and education expenses paid for by a trust, rather than simply handing over all of the assets to a young child or teenager, will be comforting to most parents. At this point, the trustee could be someone older and more responsible. Then, when the children reach a certain age, they can take control of the trust and their inheritance themselves.

If this has not been set up prior to death, part of the estate can still be transferred into a new trust to be held for the benefit of minor children. For example, if a husband dies, the wife could transfer part of the estate into a new trust and through that trust the income derived can be directed to the minor children at ordinary marginal tax rates (i.e. the first $6,000 is tax-free). However, it must take place within three years of the death of the husband.

> **Note:** *the trustee of a testamentary trust needs to be given sufficient discretion to distribute income and capital as he/she feels will be in the best interest of the beneficiaries.*

The tax benefits to the beneficiaries of a testamentary trust as mentioned earlier are extremely important, especially where children are concerned, making this structure an effective structure with which to minimise the tax that would otherwise be payable.

To demonstrate the tax implications that can apply to the beneficiaries of a Will let me show you an example:

Example:

A man dies and leaves an estate that earns $100,000 in income each year. He has a wife and two children who each receive an equal portion of his assets. The money is therefore distributed as:

Wife	$ 33,334
Child 1	$ 33,333
Child 2	$ 33,333
Total	$ 100,000

If this is the only money each of them earns in the financial year, through a normal 'inter vivos' trust (a trust formed during your lifetime), the children would be taxed at the highest marginal rate of 45% (excluding the Medicare Levy).

This means the tax payable on the $100,000 income would be as follows:

Example:

Tax payable on $100,000 through a normal 'inter vivos' trust:

Wife	$ 2,875
Child 1	$ 15,000
Child 2	$ 15,000
Total	$ 32,875

However, had the Will been set up with a testamentary trust, the children would have been taxed at adult rates which means their tax-free threshold would be increased to $18,200 and the adult rate rates would apply as follows:

Example:

Tax payable through a testamentary trust with the children taxed at adult rates:

Wife	$ 2,875
Child 1	$ 2,875
Child 2	$ 2,875
Total	$ 8,625

Tax savings of $24,250

As you can see, the tax saving is substantial, $24,250. Furthermore, when the wife dies, there are no costs to transfer the assets to the children because the assets remain the property of the trust.

Another reason for establishing this type of structure, is to try to ensure that 'in-laws" or estranged family members do not have access to a family's wealth. A common type of trust that is used to keep assets within a family is a 'bloodline™ trust'. This type of structure ensures that capital is retained by the bloodline (as determined by you and can include your children, siblings and even cousins). Anyone who does not have a blood link to you, such as a brother-in-law or spouse of your child, cannot gain access to the assets. This may or may not be relevant to your situation, but does give you that added protection in case of a nasty divorce of one of your family members.

For more information about trusts and asset protection see my book 'Asset Protection Secrets of a Real Estate Millionaire'

Inherited Property

The Capital Gains Tax implications have been explained in greater detail in Chapter 11.

Chapter 17

Investing overseas

The Australian Income Tax Act is extremely far reaching, stretching way beyond Australia's own shores, having tentacles greater than the North Pacific Giant Octopus when it comes to overseas investments. Moreover, the Australian Tax Office is also relatively more savage than the Tax Offices in most other countries around the world.

Basically, any foreign income earned by an Australian tax resident (which means you live in this country for more than 183 days), needs to be declared on their Australian tax return regardless of its source, county of origin or nature of income. While that is a very broad statement, there are exceptions to the rule which are very detailed as well as very complex.

Tax Secrets of a Real Estate Millionaire

An Australian individual either investing overseas in real estate (or anything else for that matter) or earning foreign income from pensions, contracts or business dealings etc., will be assessed on that income on their Australian Income Tax return. They will of course also have to abide by the Income Tax laws of the country from which they earned the income. For instance if they had an investment property in the UK or the United States of America, which earned income, they would have to lodge a tax return in that country. They would be taxed on the income or the profit made from the ownership of the property in that country according to their Income Tax laws. Then back in Australia, they would also have to declare this same income and any relevant expenses against that income in their Australian tax return.

Now, that may sound like they are being double-taxed, but it is really not that bad.

You will get an offset in your Australian tax return for tax paid, for instance in the UK or USA, where the property is situated, provided Australia has a double tax agreement with that country. For a list of countries Australia has a tax treaty with, see Appendix K. So you end up paying approximately the same tax as you would if you had earned the income in Australia.

Let's expand on that a little bit. Let's assume the tax rate in the country where the property is located, is 20 cents in the dollar and your rate back here in Australia is 30 cents in the dollar. What would happen, is that you would lodge your tax return in the other country and pay the 20% tax in that country. Then back here in Australia, you would declare the same income and the same expenses against that income and state that you have already paid 20% tax in the foreign country. Whilst the tax offset is not a direct credit for the 20% tax paid, you do get an offset for this tax in your Australian tax return.

See www.ato.gov.au/foreigntaxoffset for more detailed information.

Tax Secrets of a Real Estate Millionaire

Conversely, if the tax rate in the other country is say 60%, like it is in some places like Denmark, then you would be taxed in that country at the 60% but then in Australia you would get a credit for that 60% tax. So if your tax rate in Australia is 30%, you would then have a foreign tax credit that could be offset against other income.

Now, the types of countries that I am talking about when it comes to foreign investment are those countries with which Australia has a 'double tax agreement' (refer Appendix K). If Australia doesn't have a double tax agreement with a country and they are usually the tax haven countries like Vanuatu, Belize and Canary Islands etc., then no recognition of any taxes would be taken into account should any taxes be paid in that country.

Tax scams and tax havens

While we are on the topic of tax havens, let's explore that a little more. Several years ago there was an influx of foreign tax schemes which originated out of tax havens. Many of them involved pseudo companies in that country which operated with nominee directors. A nominee director is simply someone that puts their hand up to be a director for that company while you retain control. What is really happening behind the scenes, is that the Australian investor (you) has a contract or a secret agreement with an individual (usually an accountant or solicitor) in the country in which you are doing business, that says that they are the real owner and controller of the company in that country, and therefore the controller of any of the investments or assets that this company owns.

This is clearly a sham, and the Australian Tax Office has spent millions of dollars tracking down and investigating these types of tax scams.

I remember a ridiculous case several years ago when an Australian plumber decided that he would open an IBC (International Business Company) out of Vanuatu. He said that he was using his Vanuatu company to do all of his administration and invoicing, and he was trying to say that all of his income earned as a plumber in Australia, because it was being invoiced and controlled out of Vanuatu, was totally tax-free in Australia. Of course, Vanuatu is one of the tax havens in the world and doesn't have any Income Tax. Clearly this guy got hammered by the Australian Tax Office as it didn't stand up to any of the foreign investment rules, and it was clearly determined that it was a contravention of the Australian Tax Office, a tax scam, and therefore heavily penalised. In some instances these rulings can quite often carry a gaol term associated with the misdemeanour.

Whilst the legislation is complex, in broad terms the test for whether income needs to be declared or not comes down to a few simple rules:-

1. Where does the ownership actually lie? Does it lie with an Australian tax resident? (I say tax resident as even a non-Australian resident can be a tax resident of Australia because this is where they reside more than 183 days of the year and therefore are captured under the tax residency laws).

2. Where does the central management of the company actually lie? Again if this lies back here in Australia with an Australian tax resident, the company or entity will be deemed to be an Australian entity for tax purposes and therefore be required to pay taxes here in Australia.

Many tax havens and international structuring companies put all sorts of claims on how to avoid tax in Australia. The fact is that 99.9% of the time they are wrong. Quite often, the nominee directors, particularly in places like the Bahamas and South America, when under investigation, turn out to be dead or nonexistent people. The whole practice is really very dangerous as you have no come back or recourse if something goes wrong.

I remember meeting with a barrister in the USA who was promoting foreign tax structures primarily to Americans, however his market didn't preclude Australians and other nationalities. After quite a lot of alcohol consumption (on his part not mine), his conversation started to become quite liberal and when I questioned him on how holeproof the legislation was in the particular Caribbean tax haven that he was representing, he revealed that monies could quite easily be withheld, recouped, transferred, and even hidden or taken away; effectively stolen from the investors. To put it in his words 'the slip of the pen' is all it would take and he was the guy who was responsible for writing 90% of the government taxation legislation on foreign investment for a small but well known Caribbean tax haven.

You often hear about the big multinationals having offices in places like the Bahamas and Costa Rica, even some of our biggest companies have been in the headlines for similar international business strategies (notice I didn't say tax strategies), even some of our partly owned government companies like Telstra. The average person might wonder how come they can get away with it but we can't?

Well, it's not actually a matter of getting away with it, what we are talking about is coming back to those two basic rules of central management and ownership. Ownership may well be held, with the ultimate company head office being an Australian company, but the central management and control of international business endeavours in these cases are genuinely in those countries. It is not a case of having a pseudo phone number that is being answered by a telephonist with the company name should somebody ring up and there really is no business being conducted there; therefore a sham. These companies are large international companies with genuine business interests overseas that genuinely have business offices with real people, doing real work. This is very different from the case of the plumber trying to invoice out of Vanuatu, which is why they can then be taxed (or not taxed in the case of a tax haven), in those countries, and not necessarily be taxed on that income here in Australia.

Tax Secrets of a Real Estate Millionaire

Overseas investments and Capital Gains Tax

When it comes to real estate, the most common question asked is, "What if I invest in a country where there is no Capital Gains Tax? Surely so long as I don't bring the money back, I don't have to pay any Capital Gains Tax on any gains that I make on properties sold in that country, right?"

Well, actually no. Once again, any structure set up will be deemed to be an Australian tax structure and therefore taxed under the Australian tax legislation, if it cannot be classified as an exemption from one of the two prior rules of thumb, ownership and central management.

> "ask yourself what another person's benefits and qualifications are for giving you advice; are they selling you a tax structure for a fee?"

If there is no foreign country connection with no real foreign country ownership or foreign central management in the form of directorship, trusteeships, control etc., then the income, whether it be capital gain, operational income or from rents, will be taxed in Australia. Therefore, Capital Gains Tax is payable on the sale of the property.

When you start investigating overseas investing you will come across contrary advice to mine. However, you really need to look at who is providing you with the information. Ask yourself what their benefits and qualifications are for giving you that information. Are they selling you a tax structure for a fee?

In the case of New Zealand for example, quite often trust structures are set up with nominee directors of corporate trustees who are usually New Zealand resident accountants or solicitors. The accountants and solicitors generally know their own country's tax legislation and asset protection laws quite well, and they assume, incorrectly, that the Australian Tax Act is similar to their own. The fact is that the Australian Tax Act is far more aggressive when it comes to foreign income than most other westernised countries.

For example, a New Zealand resident settlor and trustee of a trust (and of course in New Zealand you actually need to have an independent trustee or an independent trustee alongside your personal trustee) makes the trust a New Zealand resident trust for tax purposes. Therefore, under New Zealand law, any capital gain derived from the sale of an investment property would not be taxable. But let's take it back on shore to Australia. If the underlying beneficiaries, central management and control, actually lie with Australian tax residents, then the trust would be treated as an Australian trust and any capital gains would be deemed to be earned in an Australian trust and therefore, assessable under the Australian Taxation Act.

The situation starts to get a little more cloudy when the Australian tax resident genuinely has family or joint-venture partners who are tax residents of New Zealand. These New Zealand tax residents can then fulfill the residency roles for trustee and settlor and therefore the trust is genuinely a New Zealand trust for tax purposes and would not fall under the realms of the Australian Taxation Act. Therefore, any capital gain made from the sale of an investment property would be tax-free provided the distribution is not made to an Australian resident for tax purposes.

It is wise to be a little bit careful of the New Zealand tainting rules which basically encompass most manufactured growth strategies such as developing subdivisions and even serial renovation.

I will make one more cautionary statement - **just having a New Zealand address won't cut it**. What you have to think of is, if you were subject to a tax audit and you were sitting across the table from a tax auditor, would your structure stand the test? Don't be fooled by tax scam sellers who have a vested interest in selling you a tax structure!

So, when can I only be taxed in the foreign country and not have the income deemed to be Australian income? Surely the fact that I choose to live in this beautiful country shouldn't compromise the amount of tax I have to pay on worldwide income?

Well, there's a lot of political issues that start to come into play even down to some of the simpler ones like, if you choose to live here, regardless of where your income is earned, you should be taxed here, because here is where you collect the benefits of the Australian lifestyle as we know it, including all the infrastructure like roads, hospitals, schools, etc.

Political issues aside, there has been a loosening of the rules for foreign income in recent years. Since July 2004, foreign income rules in Australia have definitely relaxed, and the rules regarding countries with similar tax regimes to Australia, which are called 'broad taxed countries' or 'listed countries', have been broadened significantly. The Tax Office has introduced a foreign accruals system which was designed to combat profit sheltering by foreign companies and trusts in low tax countries which are controlled by Australian tax residents.

Chapter 18

Planning for retirement; superannuation

Retirement is something a lot of people look forward to. It is that point in life where one finally gets to stop working and enjoy the fruits of their labours, relaxing, travelling or toiling away in their gardens or workshops, doing the things that they have always wanted to do, but never had the time.

Unfortunately, most people don't really start to think about retirement until they hit about 45-50, which is a shame, because when they really should start thinking about retirement is as early as their first job. Consideration at this time will give them a much better result in retirement. Consequently, many people, as they move closer to retirement, realise that they have underestimated what their needs may be, if they have estimated their needs at all, and then suddenly try to save their nest egg in the last few years as if they were cramming for an exam at uni!

So let's look at some strategies by which you can take advantage of some of the government incentives put in place to help pending retirees accumulate retirement wealth.

Superannuation

Most people these days are familiar with superannuation. Anyone who has ever worked for anyone over the last 20 years would have had some form of superannuation paid, but when someone thinks about superannuation it is normally just this far out thing into the future that is controlled by somebody else, that they don't know anything about and they feel they have very little to do with.

The government has its own set of problems; with a generation of 'baby boomers' set to hit retirement age in a few years. They have had to face the realisation that they are not going to be able to afford all of their pensions. So, in an effort to combat this predicament, they are doing everything they can to encourage people to start funding their own retirement, and in turn have created a lot of incentives to do so.

Tax offsets

Tax offsets reduce the amount of tax that you actually owe to the Tax Office. It is different to deductions in the way that the offsets are calculated on the tax that you actually have to pay rather than your taxable income.

There are three offsets that may apply to the retiree:-

1. Low Income Offset
2. Self-funded Retiree Offset
3. Mature-aged Offset

Tax Secrets of a Real Estate Millionaire

Depending on what applies to your situation, tax offsets can be applied concurrently. Firstly, a **low income offset** could be applied, then as a self-funded retiree there may be additional benefits where tax payable from income from interest, dividends or investments could trigger this offset. Then, if you are over a certain age and you have a certain level of income, once again it could trigger an offset. So finally, you could end up with $1,500 worth of offsets applied against your taxable dollars.

Let's explore this a little bit more.

Let's say for example, that Peter is a self funded retiree of pension age and he earns $30,000 a year. The income threshold for $30,000 is $18,200 leaving a balance of $11,800 that is taxed at 15%. This means that the tax owed will be $1,770. Because Peter is under a certain threshold of income, the Tax Office gives him the Low Income Offset of $1,500. So now all he owes is $270.

If part of his $30,000 income has come from interest or dividends as a self-funded retiree, he is also able to claim the Senior Australian Tax Offset. This offset is $2,230 so it reduces the $270 to zero.

Example:

Income	$30,000
Tax Threshold	$ 18,200
Taxable Income	$ 11,800
Tax Payable	$ 1,770
(15% marginal tax rate)	
Less:	
Low Income Offset	$ 1,500
Self-funded Retiree Offset	$ 2,230
Total Offsets	$ 3,730
After Offsets Tax Payable	$ zero

Finally, there is the **Mature-aged Offset** applicable to retirees over 55 who earn less than $63,000 to a maximum of $500.

Co-contributions

The government, recognising the need to encourage income earners to make contributions to their superannuation long before their retirement, has introduced additional incentives to income earners in the way of co-contribution subsidies.

Basically, if an employee contributes $1,000 from their after-tax dollars into their superannuation fund, the government would co-contribute up to $500. Although this is not a new initiative, where initially these subsidies only applied to wage earners, they now apply to everyone, self employed or otherwise.

To be eligible for the super co-contribution you would need to answer yes to all of the following:

- You made one or more eligible personal super contributions to your super account during the financial year

- You pass the two income tests

- Your total income for the financial year is less than the higher income threshold ($48,516 for 2013-14)

- 10% or more of your total income comes from eligible employment-related activities or carrying on a business, or a combination of both

- You were less than 71 years old at the end of the financial year

- You lodged your tax return for the relevant financial year.

Your maximum super co-contribution depends on your income. If your income for the 2014–15 financial year is $34,488 or less, for every $1 you personally pay into your super, the government will pay you 50 cents. As your income increases above $34,488, the amount the government contributes reduces for every $1 you earn up to $49,488.

Self-managed fund contribution limits

There are age based limits to what can be contributed to superannuation funds by employers and employees in any one financial year, and it is important to adhere to those limits as breaches can result in severe penalties that could end up negating any benefits the contributor may otherwise have been entitled to.

> Up to age 49: Limited to $30,000 p.a
> Aged 49 and over (from 30/6/2014): Limited to $35,000 p.a

Additionally, you can contribute another $180,000 per year non-concessional (after tax money) and can take advantage of a 3 year grouping arrangement which allows you to claim all 3 years together in the first year ($540,000), but then you can't put any more in for the next 2 years.

The onus is on the employee to keep track of what they are contributing to super and that applies not only to their own contributions, but to their employer's contributions as well.

> "the key is to make sure that you keep track of what is being contributed into super; your contributions and your employers contributions"

The repercussions for over-contributing to your superannuation fund results in the contributions automatically being treated as non-concessional contributions. If the excess is above the non-concessional limits and the member leaves the excess in the fund will continue to be taxed at the top marginal tax rate (46.5%), excess contributions may be refunded back to the you and taxed at your marginal tax rate with a excess concessional contributions charge. Check with your super specialist for more detailed information.

There are some fairly complex rules with regards to these additional contributions, so I guess the key is to make sure that you keep track of what is being contributed - your contributions **and** your employer's contributions.

Self-managed versus managed

Over the last decade, managing your own superannuation fund has become a popular strategy, and an option that generally anyone can take advantage of, with the exception of government employees. While managing your own superannuation fund takes time and skill, it can reap returns that you may not have otherwise had, if managed through a traditional managed fund.

When you set up your own super fund, you essentially become the controller of your fund. The fund can have a maximum of 4 members, and every member must be a trustee or director of a corporate trustee company (except in the case of a minor where a parent or guardian can act on their behalf until they are 18). Single member superannuation funds must have a corporate trustee or a relative acting as a trustee with you. I prefer a corporate trustee in all cases.

In a recent case, the Shail Case, the courts upheld the responsibility of the trustee even though there was no knowledge or benefit from a non-compliance. Mr and Mrs Shail were personal trustees of their superannuation fund when they were going through divorce. Mrs Shail did very nicely out of the long and bitter divorce. Mr Shail decided to play nasty, and withdrew all their superannuation money and skipped off overseas. ATO became aware of the fraud and non-compliance and took action against the trustees of the fund. Because Mr and Mrs Shail were personal trustees of the fund, both were joint and severally liable for the outstanding tax debt.

When a breach is confirmed, the penalties are horrendous. The tax office penalty totalled $3.59 million. Obviously Mrs Shail was not impressed – but none the less liable for the debt.

Had the trustees been a company, the result may have been very different.

To self-manage a superannuation fund, you must have a plan of attack, an 'investment strategy', and written minutes to show that you are investing according to your investment strategy. Additionally, the fund must be audited every year to ensure that you are indeed investing according to your investment strategies – penalties do apply if you invest outside of this. Finally, trustees new to self-managed superannuation, will also have to sign a declaration that states that they know what they are doing and that they will invest according to their investment strategy.

Once you have set up your self-managed superannuation fund and you are in the accumulation phase of your investment strategy, you will no doubt at some stage look towards real estate as part of your investment strategy.

Now, one of the great things with property is that you can now borrow money via the use of a limited recourse borrowing arrangement and a special holding trust (commonly called a bare trust) using property as leverage, and then really use this leverage to accumulate more property throughout the accumulation phase of your life. It is a strategy that can really accelerate your return, so obviously, when we are talking about whether we should be accumulating property inside superannuation or outside superannuation, real estate leverage needs to be taken into consideration as a superannuation fund has limited availability for borrowing. So let's take a closer look at that.

Tax Secrets of a Real Estate Millionaire

Borrowing in super funds

For a while, there was a school of thought that an individual, as 'tenants in common' with their super fund, could go out and buy a property. As tenants in common, the individual would own a specific portion of the property, for instance 60%, and the super fund would then own 40%. In the individual's part of the tenants in common, if the bank was happy with the arrangement, they may allow the individual to borrow money and only take security on the 60%, and in this case it was then okay to borrow with a super fund. However, traditionally, banks don't like to do this, and therefore it is not a strategy that is often worth pursuing.

So a better strategy to pursue would be this:-

If the individual has equity in a property (for instance, their principal place of residence), they set up a unit trust structure with a piggy bank trust; a simple discretionary trust, and use the equity from the property to lend the piggy bank trust 'x' amount of dollars, say it is $200,000. This piggy bank trust then uses this money to subscribe for 200,000 units at $1 each in the unit trust.

If a property becomes available that the trust wants to buy and for example, that property is $300,000, the remaining $100,000 can be accessed from the self-managed super fund by way of the super fund purchasing 100,000 units from the unit trust at $1 each also. By doing this, the unit trust now has the $300,000 and it can go out and buy that property. In this instance, the individual has taken advantage of leveraging without the unit trust being associated with the super fund itself. The property in the unit trust remains unencumbered and can't ever be used as security for any borrowing.

However, although this strategy does work, in reality it is an ineffective use of the leverage of that individual's home. The reason is that the trust could have borrowed that money anyway. Not only that, it could have borrowed a lot more, maybe even as much as $1,000,000 for the same amount of equity being used. So rather than having only that $300,000 accumulating value and earning income it could have had $1,000,000 worth of property accumulating income and value. So realistically, although it can be done, this is a non-aggressive strategy.

There are ways in which this strategy can be made to work depending on the individual.

Someone I know who does commercial properties, has a separate unit trust for each property that he buys and always does a joint venture with his piggy bank trust. Progressively he increases the value in his super fund through acquiring units in the other trusts. Because of the inhouse asset rules, if the trust was geared, he couldn't do it at all, but as the unit trust is not geared, it falls outside those inhouse asset rules, so progressively the super fund can acquire those other units from the original piggy bank trust even though the lending is still there. So basically, the income generated in the trust is being contributed to the super fund, and the super fund is using this money to buy back the units from the joint venture partner.

This is a very non aggressive strategy, but it is probably a good strategy for people who don't have a lot of equity outside their superannuation and want to access the superannuation fund money. This can be useful when you are doing a joint venture, and you have a self-managed super fund, and you would like to do a quick renovation that you will flip, as it can help you get going a lot quicker. Additionally, if you know someone else that has a super fund and they are not related to you then you can both subscribe to the units in the unit trust through your superannuation funds and that unit trust can now borrow. In this instance, this only applies because they are not related (3 generations or through business) and no related party has a controlling stake ie owns more than 50% of the units.

Where previously you could not borrow through a superannuation fund other than through options such as instalment warrants as non-recourse loans, new rulings have in fact broadened superannuation laws to include property and the ability to borrow through the use of a 'bare trust'.

A **bare trust** is a trust where the self-managed superannuation fund is absolutely the only entitled beneficiary. This means that there are no other beneficiaries to the trust.

Through the bare trust, the self-managed superannuation fund can borrow to buy the property, from a bank or lender, but it is the trustee of the bare trust that retains the title of the property until the final installment is paid. The superannuation fund can in turn rent the property, receive the rents, and pay the interest on the loan to the lender. Should the trustee decide a few years down the track that the property hasn't performed as well as they had hoped, they can either sell the property or quit the loan, where it then becomes the resonsibilty of the lender to sell the property and pay out the loan. If the situation occurs that lender is to sell the property due to default on the loan then the lender only has recourse over the property asset itself and no further recourse over the other assets of the self managed superannuation fund.

Alternatively, should the property perform well and you sell it to receive the profits, the profits of the property would then be returned to the superannuation fund and be required to pay tax according to its tax rate which would be effectively ten cents in the dollar while in accumulation phase and tax free if sold once the fund had moved into pension phase.

Should the property in the bare trust be negatively geared, the super fund would have to have an income from other sources to be able to take advantage of the loss – you cannot count on future contributions into the fund, it has to be offset against actual earnings.

So these are the ways that the new rulings on self-managed superannuation funds have allowed for money in these funds to be utilised. Remember that there are strict guidelines that need to be adhered to, and failing to do so can result in severe penalties to the investor. At all times when dealing with superannuation and especially complex strategies as above I recommend you seek expert advice from a licensed advisor that specialises in self managed superannuation and property transactions.

Tax Secrets of a Real Estate Millionaire

In specie transfers

At some point in your retirement strategy, you may have amassed considerable assets, and nearing retirement, you may wish to transfer some of these assets 'in kind' to your superannuation fund. This is called an 'in specie' contribution. 'In specie' contributions are an asset contribution rather than a cash contribution, and must come in under the contribution limits.

However, there are restrictions. These restrictions include residential properties. A self-managed super fund cannot acquire an asset from a member unless it's one of the following. It is a share, a life insurance policy, or a Business Real Property. If the property is the actual commercial property rather than a premises from which a business is run, this could be bought by the superannuation fund, because it is commercial - Business Real Property.

For superannuation contributions from small business events, there is an indexed lifetime limit of $1.355 million for 2014-2015.

Here is an example:

In 2014-15, Sam, aged 58, sells an active asset used in his small business. Sam has owned the business for 15 years and qualifies for the CGT 15-year exemption. The proceeds from sale are $1.405 million and the capital gain of $350,000 is disregarded. It is still 2014-15 and assuming that Sam wishes to contribute the entire capital proceeds to his superannuation fund. If he has not previously made any superannuation contributions and used his CGT cap, he could elect to contribute $1.355 million under the CGT cap exemption and have the remaining $50,000 count towards his non-concessional contributions cap.

This would allow him to make an additional $130,000 non-concessional contribution in the year without exceeding his non-concessional contributions cap or $490,000, using the "bring forward" option.

Contributions of commercial properties 'in specie' can be made into superannuation provided they fall within the maximum age limits, business limits and small business exception limits.

Prior to making 'in specie' transfers, the best strategy is to take advantage of all of the other government incentives such as co-contributions, and use your superannuation fund to accumulate wealth.

It is worth remembering that it does actually contravene the Superannuation Act if restricted 'in specie' transfers are made such as the transfer of a residential property and there are penalties involved, not excluding gaol terms. The penalties can mean that the superannuation fund can end up being taxed at 46.5%, not just the earnings but the whole amount sitting in the super fund simply because you have contravened the Act.

Nearing retirement

Let's assume we are nearing retirement and we are trying to get as much into superannuation as possible. You might ask, why are we doing this? There are a number of reasons. Through the latest overhaul in superannuation rules, it has become a very attractive place to be from say, 55 years onwards. One of the reasons is because there is no longer a 'clawback' for bankruptcy. So if you have put contributions into your superannuation fund in good faith throughout your lifetime, and also excess contributions leading up to age 60, if something happens to you outside of your superannuation fund, the fund is safe as a bankruptcy trustee cannot access these funds. It is probably one of the better asset protection vehicles available.

Another reason is that once you are over 60 years of age, the components of the superannuation fund all become tax-free. The earnings on pensions also become tax-free, so you can have a situation where if you still want to work, you can set up a transition to retirement income stream which allows you to take a minimum sum out of your superannuation fund or up to 10% of your balance and still be working.

So, if you had a large balance in your superannuation fund, you could apply a two phase strategy. The first phase would be the accumulation phase where you might be salary sacrificing your income from your employer up to $50,000. The second phase would be drawing from your pension up to $50,000 tax-free. By doing this, you are only paying the 15% contributions tax on the income that you have salary sacrificed.

Overall, the general rule is that as you get closer to 60, you should be contributing as much as possible into superannuation. This way you can take advantage of the tax-free pension component as well as all the other tax concessions which will ultimately result in prosperous, well planned, and financially stress free retirement.

Life insurance policies

One final thing to keep in mind with your retirement strategy, is life insurance policies. Most managed superannuation funds have built in life insurance policies, which in the case of a rollover will cease to exist once the fund has been closed. So if you have a self-managed superannuation fund, it is worth keeping a small sum in existing funds from which you are rolling over, to keep the fund open, and thereby keep the insurance policy valid.

A few years back, I was chatting to a friend of mine at a barbeque. He was a mining engineer, and through the mining companies he had worked for over the years, he had a number of superannuation funds. He was in the process of setting up his own self-managed superannuation fund and was telling me how he was about to rollover all of his super funds. He also happened to mention that he had had a bit of a cancer scare, at which point I mentioned that he probably shouldn't rollover the whole fund as he would lose his life insurance policy. Because he had had a cancer scare, it was unlikely that any insurance companies would reinsure him were he to give up those policies.

So it was just as well I chatted to him before he had rolled the entire sum into his superannuation. This way, he left enough money in the fund to keep his life insurance policies valid and rolled over the rest. Had he rolled over the entire balance, then his insurance policies would have become invalid and having had a cancer scare in the past he would have had next to no chance of being able to establish a new life insurance policy.

Unfortunately, this is something that people usually only find out after the event, once their policies have been cancelled and they are unable to find a new insurer, and at a point where it can't be undone.

This chapter on superannuation has been written with the helpful advice of Clint Ducat from Investor Advisory Network.
 www.investorsuccessnetwork.com.au

Chapter 19

What to do at the end of the financial year; record keeping

Record keeping is essential to meeting your tax obligations. Furthermore, good record keeping will not only help you meet these obligations, but will also save you time and money that you may have otherwise missed out on, in the way of tax-deductions, simply because you have not met the requirements of the Tax Office in terms of record keeping. It will also help you to know exactly where you are at with your finances at any time, helping you to monitor stock, income and expenditure.

The Tax Office requirements are that records should generally be kept for five years, so that is five years after any transaction or expense, or the completion of any given project. Or in the case of real estate, five years after a property is sold, even if that property has been owned for longer, for Capital Gains Tax purposes. The records must be in English, or readily convertible, and they must be relevant to the income and expenditure to which they are applied. Your records will also need to show how you determined the figures that you have declared on your tax return.

If you do not keep adequate records, the Tax Office, in the case of an audit, may require you to pay back the money that you have claimed as deductions, and even impose penalties and criminal charges in extreme cases, so keeping good records certainly has its incentives!

The end of the financial year

So the end of the financial year has come around, and it is once again time to prepare all of your income earning information to take to your accountant so that your tax return can be calculated and lodged. In Australia, the financial year is a period of 12 months that starts on the 1 July and ends on the 30 June, so a tax return is based on the income and expenditure incurred by the taxpayer during this period of time.

Visiting your accountant

It is the job and duty of any good accountant to reduce a client's taxation liability by claiming all legal deductions and structuring the client in the most tax efficient manner. Your accountant does need some help from you to be able to save you tax. It is your job to keep adequate records, communicate your dreams and intentions for the years ahead, and to have a broad understanding of what you are able to claim, to make sure you are keeping the right records.

By now, having reached the final chapter in this book, you will have sufficient knowledge to know what records to keep, know when it is appropriate to seek additional professional help, and if your current advisors know what they are talking about or if you have outgrown their area of expertise.

As a property investor, you have chosen to specialise in one particular field – it is to your advantage to deal with professionals who also specialise in that field.

Interim visits to your accountant

It is a common misconception for many to only visit their accountant once the financial year is over and by doing that, many taxpayers miss the opportunity to put into place some effective strategies by which to reduce their tax, and end up paying much more tax than they need to.

For this reason, I can't stress enough the importance of interim visits to your accountant, especially around that April/May time of year, to have a pre-year-end review. The purpose of this review is to look at the income and expenditure that you have incurred thus far, and what expenses you or your business are likely to incur over the next year.

At this point, it can be decided whether or not it would be tax effective to bring some of these expenses forward so that you can take advantage of deductions this financial year and thereby lower the tax payable. There may have been maintenance and repairs that needed to be done to your investment properties, or you may have sold that property to offset some of the losses against your capital gains. There might be expenses such as rent or lease payments or even interest on loans that you could prepay for the next 12 months, or you might even take advantage of some business related seminars to help further your knowledge and reduce your taxable income in the process. All of these things can make a huge difference to the tax payable on your income.

Conversely, had you waited until the end of the financial year, it would have been too late to put any of these strategies into place and you may have ended up paying much more tax, one, by being in a higher tax bracket than you needed to be and two, by not being able to take advantage of the deductions.

This is where good record keeping will come into play, as if you have been diligent in keeping your records, everything you need will be close at hand and will maximise your efficiency and ability to do these things.

Asset and ownership registers

If you own a property for fifteen years, you have to keep all records pertaining to that property for at least twenty years. That's a long time to keep renovation receipts, Stamp Duty particulars, costs of purchase, searches etc., and even how much depreciation you may have claimed on tax returns years ago. It is for this reason that an asset and ownership register can be extremely useful. It will help you, the investor, keep the documentation that you need to calculate and minimise your tax obligations. You can set up your own asset register, but there are some comprehensive ready-made asset registers available so that you can be sure that nothing is left out. It will help to 'audit-proof' you and your records from any tax audit.

For more information see my website for 'Insider Tax Secrets Compendium – Asset and Ownership Register:
www.dymphnaboholt.com

Assessment checklist

Once your tax return has been prepared by your accountant, it is important to double check the assessment to make sure that all the information provided is correct and complete.

Be sure to retain pay slips and invoices, passbooks and other investment information, and check these against your payment summary and other records, so that you pay tax only on the income earned during that financial year.

Sometimes there can be mistakes, as simple as a decimal point in the wrong place that can mean a difference of hundreds of dollars, so check your assessment carefully once it has been issued by the Tax Office and make sure you receive full credit for:-

- PAYG withheld from salary and wages

- PAYG instalments (check the figure is correct)

- dependant and other tax offsets

- check Withholding Tax withheld on investments due to the Tax File Number not being quoted

- imputation credits on franked dividends

Those with private health insurance cover are entitled to a tax offset based on 30% of the premiums paid. This is based on the actual amount of premiums paid up to June 30^t. If you did not claim it as a reduction in your premiums, your private health insurance fund will provide you with details of the amount against which you can claim in your tax return.

Make sure that you declare all of your interest, rent and dividend income. The Tax Office receives complete details from all companies and financial institutions of interest and dividends paid during the income year. That information is matched by computer against the declared income in your return, so it is important not to leave any of this information out. Remember, ignorance is not an excuse.

Finally, make sure you retain receipts and records including travel and expense diaries and log books used to work out the deductions derived in your assessment in case of an audit. These records must be kept for 5 years.

Tax audits

Since taxes were first introduced into our legal system, the onus on providing proof has been with the taxpayer to show their right to claim a deduction and justify their income. The Tax Office is responsible for collecting this revenue and making sure that the taxpayers pay the correct amount of tax.

A tax audit is an examination by the Tax Office of your lodgements to ensure that you have indeed declared all of the assessable income that you have received and that you are in fact entitled to the deductions and tax offsets that you have claimed on your tax return.

There are a number of ways in which tax audits are conducted, varying in complexity. Some audits may take place without you, the taxpayer, being aware. Information is cross referenced with banks and financial institutions on interest earned, Centrelink payments and other sources, to see whether or not you have declared this income on your tax return.

Sometimes an audit may be a simple line of enquiry asking you to provide further information or verification of your claims or alternately, you may have a tax officer visit you and ask to view your records.

Audit insurance can be taken out to cover the extra costs of going through an audit, costs such as bookkeeping, accounting fees etc., and of course the premiums are tax-deductible.

Tax Secrets of a Real Estate Millionaire

What do you do if the tax auditor wants to come to visit?

So, you have received a letter from the Tax Office stating that an auditor would like to make a friendly visit, and although your first inclination would be to say that you are going on a long extended holiday, that is not really an option, and providing that you have been honest on your lodgements, there is no real need for panic. The Tax Office may wish to conduct either a **review** or an **audit**. A **review** will usually be conducted to check for errors and help correct these. At this point, if it appears that you may not have been entirely forthcoming with your tax return, it may then be decided by the Tax Office to take the next step and conduct an audit. Should you yourself become aware of any errors during the process of the review, now is the time to tell the Tax Office as they will take this into consideration and significantly reduce any penalties that may otherwise have been imposed.

An **audit** is a little more comprehensive than a review and the Tax Office examines documents in greater detail and if necessary, corrects any discrepancies found. It is expected that you cooperate with the auditor and provide any documentation relevant to the audit for review.

If after examination of your records it is decided by the Tax Office that there is an amount missing on your tax return, you will then receive a *'Notice of Amended Assessment'* informing you of how much to pay – this amount may also include interest and penalties. If you agree with the amended assessment, then you will have to pay this amount, but if not, well, then you will need to lodge an objection.

Once the audit has been done, you will be notified of the outcome, and your rights and obligations, and will be guided through the process by the Tax Office.

Remember, making a false or misleading statement in a tax return or keeping incorrect or false records with an intention to deceive or mislead a tax officer is a serious offence, and once again I must stress - ignorance is not an excuse.

Record keeping tips

Here are a few record keeping tips that will help you to be organised:-

- set up an efficient filing system for all of your receipts and paperwork

- keep an asset register for each of your properties

- keep a log book or a diary to record travel and home office expenses

- keep personal and business paperwork separate

- if using accounting software, update your records regularly so files are up-to-date and you don't end up spending hours doing a big catch up

- back up all of your records if using a computer and keep the backup disc in a safe place

- fill out your cheque butts correctly when you write the cheque

- make sure your records can be understood by someone other than yourself

- it is never too late to try and follow up records that have been destroyed or misplaced

- don't be afraid to ask for help!

Tax Secrets of a Real Estate Millionaire

On the following pages are some forms and checklists that may prove useful for your record keeping and filing.

I hope this book has been helpful and informative, I have a number of other books which you can review at the back of this book as well as my real estate coaching programmes which you can check out on my websites **www.dymphnaboholt.com** and **www.iloverealestate.tv**.

Remember – treat the Tax Office like your business partner and your experience with them will be a lot easier. We as a nation need to change our attitude around tax and invest for profits not investment so we can lose money so we don't have to pay as much tax (of course I am talking here about negative gearing versus positive gearing).

My adage is:
" If you are not paying tax – you are not making any money!"

Tax Secrets of a Real Estate Millionaire

To complete your budget, keep an up-to-date record of all of your financial details including such things as the following:

Personal Records

Original mortgage account   _____

Principal outstanding on mortgage   _____

Investment money

   - where is it invested?   _____

   - when does the term expire?   _____

   - The amount invested   _____

Interest due on investments   _____

Date interest due   _____

Profit due on investments   _____

Life Insurance

   - Company   _____

   - Policy number   _____

   - Surrender Values   _____

   - Bonus Payments Due   _____

Other Insurance Details, expiry dates _____

Credit Card limit   _____

Bank Information

   - Interest Rate   _____

   - Loan Details   _____

Hire Purchase

   - Company   _____

   - Amount borrowed   _____

   - End dates   _____

   - Monthly repayment amount   _____

Tax Secrets of a Real Estate Millionaire

Cash Flow Analysis

Income:
Estimated Annual Gross Rental Income _____
Other Income _____
    Total Gross Income _____
    Less Vacancy Allowance _____
    Effective Gross Income _____

Expenses:
Body Corporate Fees _____
Rates _____
Insurance _____
Water / Sewer _____
Garbage _____
Electricity _____
Licenses _____
Advertising / Letting Fees + A46 _____
Supplies _____
Maintenance _____
Lawn _____
Pest Control _____
Management (off site) _____
Management (on site) _____
Accounting / Legal _____
Miscellaneous _____
Gas _____
Telephone _____
Pools _____
Elevator _____
Budget for Replacements _____
    _____

    Total Expenses _____
    Net Operating Income _____

Debt Service:
1st Mortgage _____
2nd Mortgage _____
Total Debt Service _____

Cash Flow: _____

Checklist of Rental Property Deductions

- Accountancy fees ☐
- Acquisition and disposal costs ☐
- Advertising for tenants ☐
- Bank charges ☐
- Borrowing expenses (claimable over 5 years) ☐
- Body corporate fees ☐
- Cleaning expenses ☐
- Computer costs ☐
- Council fees ☐
- Deduction for decline in value of depreciating assets ☐
- Electricity and gas ☐
- Gardening and lawn mowing ☐
- In-house audio/ video/ internet services ☐
- Insurance ☐
- Interest on loans ☐
- Land tax ☐
- Lease document expenses ☐
- Legal expenses ☐
- Mortgage discharge expenses ☐
- Pest control ☐
- Property agent's fees and commissions ☐
- Quantity surveyor's fees ☐
- Repairs and maintenance ☐
- Replacement expenses ☐
- Secretarial and bookkeeping fees ☐
- Security fees ☐
- Servicing costs ☐
- Stationery, postage and incidental expenses ☐
- Telephone calls and rental of phone services ☐
- Tax related expenses ☐
- Travel and car expenses ☐
- Water charges ☐

Investing Entity Tax Return Checklist

Entity Name:
Investment Activity:
Income
Banks, Building Societies, Investments and Term Deposits
- ☐ Bank Statements indicating nature of each deposit and expense.

Rental Properties
- ☐ Statements of shares purchased, sold or held (with price, share number, dates purchased or sold, brokerage fees and Stamp Duty)
- ☐ Dividend Statements

Capital Gains
- ☐ Details of any capital assets acquired on or after 20 September 1985 that were sold in the tax year.
- ☐ Details of additions/improvements to assets

Other Income
- ☐ Bank statements, receipts, invoices, cashbook records of any other income

Expenses
Loans
- ☐ Statements for all loans owing by the entity, with an end of financial year balance and interest paid for the financial year

Rental Property
- ☐ Copy of purchase contract and settlement statements, including incidental costs on purchase (legals, Stamp Duty, etc.) for any new properties purchased during the year.
- ☐ Details of all expenditure incurred including supporting information (management fees, advertising, rates, gardening, insurance, etc)
- ☐ Details of any repairs, improvements, or maintenance to rental assets during the tax year.
- ☐ Tax depreciation schedule or Quantity Surveyors report per property
- ☐ Total interest paid on each loan per property
- ☐ The costs of attending any seminars related to management of rental properties including fees, travel, accommodation, meals, etc.

Share Trading
- ☐ The costs of attending seminars or courses, including fees, travel, accommodation, meals, etc
- ☐ Details of expenditure on software, home office, brokerage, etc.

Appendix A

Summary of GST status

Summary of GST status	
Transaction	**GST Treatment**
Sale of Residential Premises: Newly Built	Taxable if sold within 5 years by entity required to be registered
Sale of Residential Premises: Substantially Renovated	Taxable if sold within 5 years by entity required to be registered
Sale of Residential Premises: Not new	Input taxed regardless of whether entity is registered
Sale of Residential Land	Taxable if sold by an entity required to be registered
Rental or Residential Premises	Input taxed regardless of GST registration Status
Rental or Display Home	Input taxed regardless of GST registration Status
Expenses connected with Rental of Residential Property (insurance, repairs, agency, commission)	No input tax entitlement regardless of GST registration Status
Sale of Commercial Property	Assessable under either the margin schemes or normal GST on sale proceeds. In some circumstances could be GST exempt due to sale as a going concern.
Rental of Commercial Property	Collections exceed $75,000: taxable and entity required to be registered and GST on expenses credited. Collections less than $75,000: registration optional if entity registered then: GST to be remitted on collections offset by GST on expenses. If entity chooses not to be registered – no GST collected on rental income & no GST credits claimed on expenses.

Appendix B

Trust Capital Gains Tax rates		
Trust Structure	**50% CGT ex.***	**CGT Rate**
Company Trust	No	30%
Unit Trust	No	Marginal Tax Rate of Unit Holders
Discretionary Trust	Yes	Marginal Tax Rates of Beneficiaries
Hybrid Trust	Yes	Marginal Tax Rate of Beneficiaries or Unit Holders

* Exemption entitlement subject to ownership of the property for greater than 12 months from contract date to contract date.

Appendix C

Effective Life Tables for rental property depreciation schedule

The following table identifies the most common items in a residential rental property for which deductions can be claimed for decline in value or depreciation.

Effective Life Tables	
Asset	**Life (years)**
General Assets:	
Air Conditioning assets (excluding ducting, pipes and vents):	
Air Handling Units	20
Chillers:	
Absorption	25
Centrifugal	20
Volumetrics:	
Air-cooled	15
Water-cooled	20
Condensing Sets	15
Cooling Towers	15
Damper Motors	10
Fan Coil Units	15
Mini Split Systems up to 20KW	10
Packaged air conditioning units	15
Pumps	20
Room units	10
Air conditioning ducts, pipes and vents	See Appendix D
Cable Trays	See Appendix D
Ceiling fans	5
Clocks, electric	10
Cupboards, other than freestanding	See Appendix D
Digital video display (DVD) players	5

Asset	Life (years)
Door closers	10
Door Locks and Latches (excluding electronic code pads)	See Appendix D
Door stops, fixed	See Appendix D
Door stops, freestanding	10
Electrical assets (including conduits, distribution boards, power points, switchboards, switches and wiring)	See Appendix D
Escalators (machinery and moving parts)	20
Evaporative coolers	20
Fixed (excluding ducting and vents)	20
Portable	10
Façade, fixed	See Appendix D
Floor coverings, fixed (including cork, linoleum, parquetry, tiles and vinyl)	See Appendix D
Floor coverings (removable without damage):	
Carpet	10
Floating Timber	15
Linoleum	10
Vinyl	10
Furniture, freestanding	13 1/3
Garbage bins	10
Garbage chutes	See Appendix D
Garbage compacting systems (excl chutes)	6 2/3
Generators	20
Grease traps	See Appendix D
Gym Assets:	
Cardiovascular	5
Resistance	10
Hand dryers, electrical	10
Hand rails	See Appendix D
Heaters	
Fixed:	
Ducts, pipes, vents and wiring	See Appendix D
Electric	15
Fire Places including wood heaters	See Appendix D

Asset	Life (years)
Gas:	
Ducted central heating unit	20
Other	15
Free Standing	15
Hooks, robe	See Appendix D
Hot water systems (excluding piping):	
Electric	12
Gas	12
Solar	15
Hot water System piping	See Appendix D
Insulation	See Appendix D
Intercom assets	10
Lift wells	See Appendix D
Lifts (including hydraulic and traction lifts)	30
Lights:	
Fittings (excluding hardwired)	5
Fittings, hardwired	See Appendix D
Freestanding	5
Shades, removable	5
Linen	5
Master antenna television (MATV) assets:	
Amplifiers	10
Modulators	20
Power Sources	10
Master Antenna television (MATV) assets (excluding amplifiers, modulators and power sources)	See Appendix D
Mirrors, fixed	See Appendix D
Mirrors, freestanding	15
Radios	10
Ramps	See Appendix D
Rugs	7
Safes, fixed	See Appendix D
Sanitary fixtures, fixed (incl. soap dispensers)	See Appendix D
Satellite dishes	See Appendix D

Asset	Life (years)
Screens	See Appendix D
Shelving, other than freestanding	See Appendix D
Shutters	See Appendix D
Signs, fixed	See Appendix D
Skylights	See Appendix D
Solar powered generating system assets	20
Stereo systems incorporating amplifiers, cassettes players, compact disc players, radios and speakers)	7
Surround sound systems (incorporating audio-video receivers and speakers)	10
Telecommunication assets:	
Cordless phone	4
Distribution frames	See Appendix D
PABX computerised systems	10
Telephone hand sets	10
Television antennas, fixed	See Appendix D
Television antennas, freestanding	5
Television sets	10
Vacuum cleaners:	
Ducted:	
Hoses	10
Motors	10
Wands	10
Portable	10
Vacuum cleaners, ducted (excluding hoses, motors and wands)	See Appendix D
Ventilation ducting and vents	See Appendix D
Ventilation fans	20
Video cassette recorder systems (VCR)	5
Water pumps	20
Water tanks	See Appendix D
Window awnings, insect screens, louvres, pelmets and tracks	See Appendix D
Window blinds, internal	10
Window curtains	6
Window shutters, automatic	

Asset	Life (years)
Controls	10
Motors	10
Window shutters, automatic (excluding controls and motors)	See Appendix D
Bathroom assets	
Accessories, fixed (including mirrors, rails, soap holders and toilet roll holders)	See Appendix D
Accessories, freestanding (including shower caddies, soap holders, toilet brushes)	5
Exhaust fans (including light/heating)	10
Fixtures (including baths, bidets, tap ware toilets, vanity units and wash basins)	See Appendix E
Heated towel rails, electric	10
Shower assets (including doors, rods, screens and trays)	See Appendix D
Shower curtains (excluding curtain rods and screens)	2
Spa baths (excluding pumps)	See Appendix D
Spa bath pumps	20
Bedroom Assets	
Wardrobes, other than freestanding (incorporating doors, fixed fittings and mirrors)	See Appendix D
Fire Control Assets	
Alarms:	
Heat	6
Smoke	6
Detection and alarm systems:	
Alarm bells	12
Cabling and reticulation	See Appendix D
Detectors	20
Fire indicator panels	12
Manual call points (non-addressable)	See Appendix D
Doors, fire and separation	See Appendix D

Asset	Life (years)
Emergency warning and intercommunication systems (EWIS):	
Master emergency control panels	12
Speakers	12
Strobe lights	12
Warden intercom phone	12
Extinguishers	15
Hose cabinets and reels (excluding hoses and nozzles)	See Appendix D
Hoses and nozzles	10
Hydrant boosters (excluding pumps)	See Appendix D
Hydrants	See Appendix D
Lights, exit and emergency	See Appendix D
Pumps (including diesel and electric)	25
Sprinkler systems (excluding pumps0	See Appendix D
Stair pressurisation assets:	
A C variable speed drives	10
Pressurisation and extraction fans	25
Sensors	10
Water piping	See Appendix D
Water tanks	See Appendix D
Kitchen assets	
Cook tops	12
Crockery	5
Cutlery	5
Dishwashers	10
Fixtures (including bench tops, cupboards, sinks, tap ware and tiles0	See Appendix D
Freezers	12
Garbage disposal units	10
Microwave ovens	10
Ovens	12
Range hoods	12
Refrigerators	12
Stoves	12

Asset	Life (years)
Water filters, electrical	15
Water filters, fixed (attached to plumbing)	See Appendix D
Laundry Assets:	
Clothes dryers	10
Fixtures (including tap ware, tiles and tubs)	See Appendix D
Ironing boards, freestanding	7
Ironing boards, other than freestanding	See Appendix D
Irons	5
Washing machines	10
Outdoor Assets:	
Automatic garage doors:	
Controls	5
Motors	10
Automatic garage doors (excluding controls and motors)	See Appendix D
Barbeques	
Fixed	See Appendix D
Sliding trays and cookers	10
Freestanding barbeques	5
Bollards, fixed	See Appendix D
Car parks, sealed	See Appendix D
Carports	See Appendix D
Clotheslines	See Appendix D
Driveways, sealed	See Appendix D
Fencing	See Appendix D
Floor carpet (including artificial grass and matting)	5
Furniture, freestanding	5
Furniture, other than freestanding	See Appendix D
Garage doors (excl motors and controls)	See Appendix D
Garden awnings & shade structures, fixed	See Appendix D
Gardening watering installations:	
Control panels	5

Asset	Life (years)
Pumps	5
Timing devices	5
Gardening watering installations (excluding control panels, pumps and timing devices)	See Appendix D
Garden lights, fixed	See Appendix D
Garden lights, solar	8
Garden sheds, freestanding	15
Garden sheds, other than freestanding	See Appendix D
Gates, electrical:	
Controls	5
Motors	10
Gates (excluding electrical controls and motors)	See Appendix D
Jetties and boat sheds	See Appendix D
Letter boxes	See Appendix D
Operable pergola louvres:	
Controls	15
Motors	15
Operable pergola louvres (excluding controls and motors)	See Appendix D
Paths	See Appendix D
Retaining walls	See Appendix D
Saunas (excluding heating assets)	See Appendix D
Sauna heating assets	15
Screens, fixed (including glass screens)	See Appendix D
Septic tanks	See Appendix D
Sewage treatment assets:	
Controls	8
Motors	8
Sewage treatment assets (excluding controls and motors)	See Appendix D
Spas:	
Fixed spa assets	See Appendix D
Chlorinators	12
Filtration (including pumps)	12
Heaters (electric or gas)	15

Asset	Life (years)
Freestanding (incorporating blowers, controls, filters, heaters and pumps)	17
Swimming pool assets:	
Chlorinators	12
Cleaning	7
Filtration (including pumps)	12
Heaters:	
Electric	15
Gas	15
Solar	20
Swimming Pools	See Appendix D
Tennis Court Assets:	
Cleaners	3
Drag brooms	3
Nets	5
Rollers	3
Umpire chairs	15
Tennis court assets, fixed (including fences, lights, posts and surfaces)	See Appendix D
Security and Monitoring Assets	
Access controls Systems:	
Code pads	5
Door controllers	5
Readers:	
Proximity	7
Swipe card	3
Closed circuit television systems:	
Cameras	4
Monitors	4
Recorders:	
Digital	4
Time lapse	2
Switching units (including multiplexes)	5
Doors and screens	See Appendix D

Asset	Life (years)
Security Systems:	
Code pads	5
Control panels	5
Detectors	5
Global systems for Mobiles (GSM) units	5
Noise makers	5

Appendix D.

Capital Works

The Tax Office allows a deduction for construction expenditure on capital works. The term capital works includes buildings, structural improvements and environmental protection earthworks that are used for income producing purposes.

The right of the annual deduction depends upon the type of capital works and the date its construction is commenced.

The deduction for capital works commenced before the 1 July 1997 is dependent upon what the properties intended use was. A list of these intended uses are detailed on the following page.

Capital works intended uses table

Type of Construction	Start Date	Rate (%)	Years
Short-term traveler accommodation[5]	22/8/79 – 21/8/84	2.5	40
	22/8/84 – 17/7/85[4]	4	25
	18/7/85 – 15/9/87[6]	4	25
	16/9/87 – 26/2/92	2.5	40
	27/02/1992[4]	4	25
Non-residential income producing buildings[7]	20/7/82 – 21/8/84	2.5	40
	22/8/84 – 15/9/87[5]	4	25
	16/09/1987	2.5	40
Buildings used for eligible industrial activities	27/02/1992	4	25
Residential income producing building	18/7/85 – 15/9/87[5]	4	25
	16/09/1987	2.5	40
Income producing structural improvements	27/02/1992	2.5	40
R & D buildings	21/11/1987[5]	2.5	40
Environment protection earthworks	19/08/1992	2.5	40

---

[5] If the building is being used for another purpose, or had less than 10 accommodation units, there is:
    i.   No deduction for pre 18 July 1985 constructions;
    ii.   2.5% deduction for post 26 February 1992 constructions.

[6] Or a contract was entered into before this date.

[7] The 4% rate may apply if construction commenced after 26 February 1992 and the income producing building was used mainly for industrial activities.

Appendix E

Indexation Tables

The table below contains the entire set of index numbers to be used to September 1999, which is the date on which indexation is frozen.

CGT Indexation Tables

CGT Index Factors:	Mar	Jun	Sep	Dec
1985	-	-	71.30	72.70
1986	74.40	75.60	77.60	79.80
1987	81.40	82.60	84.00	85.50
1988	87.00	88.50	90.20	92.00
1989	92.90	95.20	97.40	99.20
1990	100.90	102.50	103.30	106.00
1991	105.80	106.00	106.60	107.60
1992	107.60	107.30	107.40	107.90
1993	108.90	109.30	109.80	110.00
1994	110.40	111.20	111.90	112.80
1995	114.70	116.20	117.60	118.50
1996	119.00	119.80	120.10	120.30
1997	120.50	120.20	119.70	120.00
1998	120.30	121.00	121.30	121.90
1999	121.80	122.30	123.40	

To calculate the index factor for CGT purposes for transaction in the 2004/2005 tax year, use this formula and round to 3 decimal places:

$$\frac{\text{Index Number for the quarter ending 30 September 1999}}{\text{Index Number for the quarter in which the expenditure was incurred}}$$

The indexation is different where the CGT asset is a share in a company or unit in a unit trust.

The indexation factor for share or trust is:

$$\frac{\text{Index Number for the quarter ending on 30 September 1999}}{\text{Index Number for the quarter in which the amount was paid}}$$

Appendix F

History of Tax Law

	The History of Tax Law	
Milestones	**Details**	**Source Documents** *(All Acts are Commonwealth unless otherwise indicated)*
1805	First import duties and charges levied in Australia to build a gaol and orphanage in Sydney	*Government and General Order, 10th March 1805, Historical Records of New South Wales, vol. 5, p. 569-570*
1819	UK legislation provides retrospectively for the Governor to levy existing duties and to levy equivalent excise on production of spirits within the colony up to 10s a gallon	*Duties in New South Wales Act 1819, chapter 114, (UK)*
1823	With the end of military government UK government gives the Governor (advised by Council) the power to tax, constrained by requirement of local purposes only	*Administration of Justice in New South Wales and Van Diemen's Land Act 1823, chapter 96, (UK)*
1825	Proclamation dated 4 February 1825 levied duties on spirits and tobacco and ad valorem tariff of 5% on foreign goods	*Historical Records of Australia, series 1, vol. xi, p. 492-493*
1851	NSW first introduces death duties. NSW levies probate and administration fees on the value of personal estate.	*Deceased Persons (Estates) Act 1851, no. 8 (NSW)*

1852-3	Introduction of gold licence fee in NSW	*Gold Fields Act 1852, no. 43 (NSW))* and *Victoria (Gold Fields) Act 1853 no. 4 (Vic)*
1877	Land tax first imposed (in Victoria) to break up large holdings	*Land Tax Act 1877, no. 575 (Vic)*
1880	First Australian Income Tax introduced with Tasmania's Withholding Tax on dividends, annuities and rents. By 1907 all States had introduced Income Tax.	*Real and Personal Estates Duties Act 1880 (43 Vic. no. 12) (Tas)*
1884	First Australian general Income Tax and land tax based on unimproved value introduced in South Australia	*Taxation Act 1884, no. 323 (SA)*
1894	Tasmania introduces general Income Tax	*Income Tax Act 1894, no. 16 (Tas)*
1895	Victoria introduces general Income Tax	*Income Tax Act 1895, no. 1374 (Vic)*
1901	Commonwealth of Australia established with Constitution giving the Commonwealth concurrent power with the states to levy taxes (section 51 (ii)) and exclusive power to impose duties of customs and excise (section 90). Uniform national tariff introduced (section 88) Customs administration for duties on imports and exports and related matters established Excise administration established for duties on manufactured goods	*Customs Act 1901 no. 6* *Excise Act 1901, no. 9*
1902	Uniform rates of customs duties set by Commonwealth on various goods sets rates of excise duties imposed on beer, spirits, starch, sugar and tobacco	*Customs Tariff Act 1902 no. 14* *Excise Tariff Act 1902 no. 11*

	Queensland introduces general Income Tax	(Income Tax Act 1902, no. 10 (Qld)
1903	WA introduces death duties on real and personal estates	Administration Act 1903, no. 13 (WA)
1910	Commonwealth introduces land tax on unimproved values. Land Tax Office (predecessor of the Australian Taxation Office) established in November within the Dept of the Treasury to administer the tax	Land Tax Act 1910 no. 21
	Commonwealth taxes private banknotes at prohibitive rates	Bank Notes Tax Act 1910 no. 14
	Commonwealth provides for financial assistance to the states under section 96 of the Constitution (grants power)	Surplus Revenue Act 1910 no. 8
1914	Commonwealth imposes death duties (national estate and succession duty)	Estate Duty Act 1914 no. 25; Estate Duty Assessment Act 1914, no. 22
1915	Commonwealth introduces personal Income Tax and tax on undistributed company profits (dividends). Name of Land Tax Office (est. 1910) changed to Taxation Office to reflect wider responsibilities	Income Tax Assessment Act 1915 no. 34
1916	Commonwealth entertainment tax introduced	Entertainments Tax Act 1916, no. 38
1918	1/2d (halfpenny) war tax levied on postage stamps. The legislation was repealed in 1920 but the increase in postage remained	Post and Telegraph Rates Act 1918, no. 24; Post and Telegraph Rates Act 1920, no. 27
1930	Commonwealth introduces 2.5% sales tax in August to offset fall in customs revenues	Sales Tax Acts and Sales Tax Assessment Acts 1930 nos 25-42

Year	Event	Legislation
1936	Unified Commonwealth and state Income Tax return introduced following recommendation of Fergusson Royal Commission (1932-34)	*Income Tax Assessment Act 1936 no. 27*
1939	Gold tax introduced	*Gold Tax Act 1939 no. 52 and Gold Tax Collection Act 1939 no. 51*
1941	War tax introduced	*War Tax Act 1941 no. 70*
	Pay-roll tax introduced to pay for child endowment	*Pay-roll Tax Act 1941 no. 3 and Pay-roll Tax Assessment Act 1941 no. 2*
	Gift duty introduced on disposition of property	*Gift Duty Act 1941 no. 53 and Gift Duty Assessment Act 1941 no. 52*
	1/2d (halfpenny) war tax levied on postage stamps. The legislation was repealed in 1949 but the increase in postage remained	*Post and Telegraph Rates Act 1941, no. 54; Post and Telegraph Rates Act 1949, no. 23;*
1942	System of uniform tax introduced by which grants to the states from the commonwealth replaced state revenue from Income Tax and state Income Taxes no longer collected	*Income Tax Act 1942, no. 23*
1944	Pay-as-you-earn (PAYE) tax system of periodic tax payments through the employer introduced for wage and salary earners by Commonwealth, with a provisional tax system introduced for non-wages and salary income	*Income Tax Assessment Act 1944, no. 3*

1950	Income Tax Assessment Act 1936 retitled as Income Tax and Social Services Contribution Assessment Act 1936	Income Tax and Social Services Contribution Assessment Act 1950, no. 48
1952	Commonwealth land tax abolished in favour of states	Land Tax Abolition Act 1952 no.81
1953	Entertainment tax abolished	Entertainments Tax Abolition Act 1953 no. 39
1965	Income Tax and Social Services Contribution Assessment Act 1936 retitled as Income Tax Assessment Act 1936	Income Tax Assessment Act 1965, no. 103
1968	Name of Taxation Office changed to Commonwealth Taxation Office	
1971	Commonwealth passes payroll tax to states after they request access to Income Tax	Pay-roll Tax (Termination of Commonwealth Tax) Act 1971 no. 76
1972	Name of Commonwealth Taxation Office changed to Australian Taxation Office	
1975	Commonwealth Taxation Review Committee recommends a broad based consumption tax etc	
1976	Queensland abolishes death and gift (estate) duties. Act takes effect from 1st January 1977. Other States follow. Through a series of amendments from 1976-1980 to the Stamp Duties Act 1920, NSW abolishes death duties. The first amendment is the Stamp Duties (Amendment) Act 1975,	Succession and Gift Duties Abolition Act 1976, no. 93 (Qld)

various Probate Duties Acts 1976-80 (Vic) |

	no. 75 and the last is the Stamp Duties (Further Amendment) Act 1980, no. 161. Abolition takes effect on or after 31/12/1981.	
	Victoria abolishes death duties	
1978	Commonwealth abolishes death and gift duties to take effect from 1 July 1979	*Estate Duty Amendment Act 1978, no. 23* and *Gift Duty Amendment Act 1978, no. 25*
	Tasmania abolishes death duties. Act is gradually applied during 1979 and 1980. Western Australia abolishes death duties	*Deceased Persons' Estates Duties (No. 2) Act 1978 (no. 49) (Tas.)* *(Death Duty Act Amendment Act 1978, no. 61 (WA)*
1979	South Australia abolishes death and gift duties (to take effect from 1st January 1980)	*Gift Duty Act Amendment Act 1979 (no. 63) (SA)*
1981	Personal Income Tax indexation abolished	*Income Tax (Assessment and Rates) Amendment Act 1981, no. 109*
1984	Medicare levy introduced 1st February 1984	*Medicare Levy Act 1983, no. 52*
1986	Capital gains tax introduced Fringe benefits tax introduced	*Income Tax Assessment Amendment (Capital Gains) Act 1986, no. 52 1999-2000.*
1997	Governments tried to 'simplify' the Income Tax Assessment Act 1936 by introducing a new act of the same name and rewriting the provisions. Both acts remain in force and must be referred to.	*Income Tax Assessment Act 1997, no. 38*
1999-2000	A 10% Goods and Services Tax was introduced gradually replacing various taxes such as sales tax. About 30 related Acts also passed (nos 56-86 of 1999). Most Acts commenced on 1 July	*A New Tax System (Goods and Services Tax) Act 1999, no. 55*

	2000	
2006	Major law reform initiative results in repeal of 68 redundant tax acts and amendments to several acts	*Tax Laws Amendment (Repeal of Inoperative Provisions) Act 2006, no. 101*
2012	Tax on profits that have been generated from non-renewable resources in Australia. Mineral Resource Rent Tax (MRRT) commencing 1st July 2012.	*Tax passed by Senate o 19th March 2012, effective 1st July 2012.*
2012	A clean energy agreement was established to reduce carbon pollution as part of an effort to combat climate change commencing 1st July 2012.	*Clean Energy Agreement on climate change.*

Appendix G

Tax rates 2013-2014

Tax rates for resident individuals 2013-2014	
Taxable income	**Tax on this income**
$0 – $18,200	Nil
$18,201 – $37,000	19c for each $1 over $18,200
$37,001 – $80,000	$3,572 plus 32.5c for each $1 over $37,000
$80,001 – $180,000	$17,547 plus 37c for each $1 over $80,000
$180,001 and over	$54,547 plus 45c for each $1 over $180,000

Tax rates for non-excepted minors 2013-2014	
Taxable income	**Tax on this income**
$0 – $416	Nil
$417 – $1,307	Nil + 66% of the excess over $416
Over $1,308	45% of the entire amount

Tax Secrets of a Real Estate Millionaire

Tax rates 2014-2015

Tax rates for resident individuals 2014-2015

Taxable income	Tax on this income
$0 – $18,200	Nil
$18,201 – $37,000	19c for each $1 over $18,200
$37,001 – $80,000	$3,572 plus 32.5c for each $1 over $37,000
$80,001 – $180,000	$17,547 plus 37c for each $1 over $80,000
$180,001 and over	$54,547 plus 45c for each $1 over $180,000

Tax rates for non-excepted minors 2014-2015

Taxable income	Tax on this income
$0 – $416	Nil
$417 – $1,307	Nil + 66% of the excess over $416
Over $1,308	45% of the entire amount

Appendix H

Real Estate Purchase Expenses - Tax Classifications

Costs	Investment	PPR
Purchasing Costs		
Real Estate Agent's Fees	Paid By Seller	Non-deductible
Finder's Fee	Capital	Non-deductible
Legal Fees	Capital	Non-deductible
Title Search	Capital	Non-deductible
Title Policy Charges	Capital	Non-deductible
Title Recording Fees	Capital	Non-deductible
Stamp Duty	Capital	Non-deductible
Surveyor's Report	Capital	Non-deductible
Building Report	Capital	Non-deductible
Pest Report	Capital	Non-deductible
Operational Cost Adjustments		
Council Rates	Deductible	Non-deductible
Insurance	Deductible	Non-deductible
Body Corporate Fees	Deductible	Non-deductible
Utilities	Deductible	Non-deductible
Financing Costs		
Legal Fees	Amortise*	Non-deductible
Valuation Fees	Amortise*	Non-deductible
Mortgage Brokers Fees	Amortise*	Non-deductible
Credit Reports	Amortise*	Non-deductible
Commitment Fees	Amortise*	Non-deductible
Loan Fees	Amortise*	Non-deductible
Mortgage Insurance Premiums	Amortise*	Non-deductible
Interest Prepayments		
Interest Paid	Deductible	Non-deductible
Prepaid Interest	Deductible	Non-deductible
GST		
See Appendix A		

* Amortised over 5 years or life of loan

Appendix I

Summary of car expense methods

	Cents per km	12% of Original Cost	1/3 of Actual Expenses	Log Book
Special Eligibility Rules	None, but limited to a claim of 5,000 kms per yr	Business & employment use must exceed 5,000 km/yr	Business & employment use must exceed 5,000 kms/yr	Car must have been owned or leased
Expense Base	Business kms	Original Value	Cost of car expenses, e.g. Fuel, tyres, service etc.	
	↓	↓	↓	↓
Calculate Deduction	Multiply by cents per km	Multiply by 12%	Multiply by 1/3	Multiply by % business use
	↓	↓	↓	↓
Must Substantiate Expenses?	No	No	Yes	Yes

---

[14] Taxpayers Australia Inc., *2006 & 2007 Tax Summary – Your plain English guide to tax.*

Appendix J

Travel claims within Australia for 2014-2015 reasonable limits

2014/15 Salary Levels below $112,610

Location	Accom.	B'fast	Lunch	Dinner	Sundry	Total
Adelaide	$157.00	$25.35	$28.55	$48.65	$18.70	$278.25
Brisbane	$201.00	$25.35	$28.55	$48.65	$18.70	$322.25
Canberra	$168.00	$25.35	$28.55	$48.65	$18.70	$289.25
Darwin	$216.00	$25.35	$28.55	$48.65	$18.70	$337.25
Hobart	$132.00	$25.35	$28.55	$48.65	$18.70	$253.25
Melbourne	$173.00	$25.35	$28.55	$48.65	$18.70	$294.25
Perth	$233.00	$25.35	$28.55	$48.65	$18.70	$354.25
Sydney	$185.00	$25.35	$28.55	$48.65	$18.70	$306.25
High Cost Country	See below	$25.35	$28.55	$48.65	$18.70	See below
Tier 2 Country Centers	$132.00	$22.70	$25.95	$44.75	$18.70	$244.10
Other Country Centers	$110.00	$22.70	$25.95	$44.75	$18.70	$222.10

2014/15 Salary Levels $112,611 - $200,290

Location	Accom.	B'fast	Lunch	Dinner	Sundry	Total
Adelaide	$208.00	$27.60	$39.10	$54.75	$26.75	$356.20
Brisbane	$257.00	$27.60	$39.10	$54.75	$26.75	$405.20
Canberra	$223.00	$27.60	$39.10	$54.75	$26.75	$371.20
Darwin	$287.00	$27.60	$39.10	$54.75	$26.75	$435.20
Hobart	$176.00	$27.60	$39.10	$54.75	$26.75	$324.20
Melbourne	$228.00	$27.60	$39.10	$54.75	$26.75	$376.20
Perth	$260.00	$27.60	$39.10	$54.75	$26.75	$408.20
Sydney	$246.00	$27.60	$39.10	$54.75	$26.75	$379.20
High Cost Country	See below	$27.60	$39.10	$54.75	$26.75	See below
Tier 2 Country Centers	$152.00	$25.35	$25.95	$50.55	$26.75	$280.60
Other Country Centers	$127.00	$24.90	$25.35	$50.55	$26.75	$255.60

2014/15 Salary Levels $200,291 and above

Location	Accom.	B'fast	Lunch	Dinner	Sundry	Total
Adelaide	$209.00	$32.55	$46.10	$64.60	$26.75	$379.00
Brisbane	$257.00	$32.55	$46.10	$64.60	$26.75	$427.00
Canberra	$246.00	$32.55	$46.10	$64.60	$26.75	$416.00
Darwin	$287.00	$32.55	$46.10	$64.60	$26.75	$457.00
Hobart	$195.00	$32.55	$46.10	$64.60	$26.75	$365.00
Melbourne	$265.00	$32.55	$46.10	$64.60	$26.75	$435.00
Perth	$299.00	$32.55	$46.10	$64.60	$26.75	$469.00
Sydney	$265.00	$32.55	$46.10	$64.60	$26.75	$435.00
Country Centres	$190 or see Table 4	$32.55	$46.10	$64.60	$26.75	See Table 4

High Cost Country Centres – Table 4

Location	Accom.	Location	Accom.
Albany (WA)	$179.00	Jabiru (NT)	$192.00
Alice Springs (NT)	$150.00	Kalgoorie (WA)	$159.00
Bordertown (SA)	$135.00	Karratha (WA)	$347.00
Bourke (NSW)	$165.00	Katherine (NT)	$134.00
Bright (VIC)	$136.00	Kingaroy (QLD)	$134.00
Broome (WA)	$233.00	Kununurra (WA)	$202.00
Bunbury (WA)	$155.00	Mackay (QLD)	$161.00
Burnie (TAS)	$149.00	Maitland (NSW)	$152.00
Cairns (QLD)	$140.00	Mount Isa (QLD)	$160.00
Carnarvon (WA)	$151.00	Newcastle (NSW)	$152.00
Castlemaine (VIC)	$133.00	Newman (WA)	$195.00
Chinchilla (QLD)	$143.00	Northam (WA)	$163.00
Christmas Island (WA)	$150.00	Northfolk Island	$329.00
Cocos (Keeling) Islands (WA)	$285.00	Orange (NSW)	$149.00
Colac (VIC)	$138.00	Port Hedland (WA)	$295.00
Dalby (QLD)	$144.00	Port Pirie (SA)	$140.00
Dampier (WA)	$175.00	Queanbeyan (NSW)	$133.00
Derby (WA)	$190.00	Roma (QLD)	$139.00
Devonport (TAS)	$135.00	Thursday Island (QLD)	$200.00
Emerald (QLD)	$156.00	Wagga Wagga (NSW)	$141.00
Exmouth (WA)	$255.00	Weipa (QLD)	$138.00
Geraldton (WA)	$175.00	Wilpena-Pound (SA)	$167.00
Gladstone (QLD)	$187.00	Whyalla (SA)	$145.00
Gold Coast (QLD)	$149.00	Wonthaggi (VIC)	$138.00
Gosford (NSW)	$140.00	Woolongong (NSW)	$136.00
Halls Creek (WA)	$199.00	Yulara (NT)	$244.00
Hervey Bay (QLD)	$157.00		
Horn Island (QLD)	$180.00		

Tier 2 Country Centres

Albury (NSW)	Goulburn (NSW)	Sale (VIC)
Ararat (VIC)	Gunneday (NSW)	Seymour (VIC)
Armidale (NSW)	Hamilton (VIC)	Shepparton (VIC)
Ayr (QLD)	Horsham (VIC)	Swan Hill (VIC)
Bairnsdale (VIC)	Innisfail (QLD)	Tamworth (NSW)
Ballarat (VIC)	Kadina (SA)	Tennant Creek (NT)
Bathurst (NSW)	Launceston (TAS)	Toowoomba (QLD)
Benalla (VIC)	Mildura (VIC)	Townsville (QLD)
Bendigo (VIC)	Mount Gambier (SA)	Tumut (NSW)
Broken Hill (NSW)	Muswellbrook (NSW)	Warnambool (VIC)
Bundaberg (QLD)	Nowra (NSW)	
Ceduna (SA)	Port Augusta (SA)	
Charters Towers (QLD)	Portland (VIC)	
Coffs Harbour (NSW)	Port Lincoln (SA)	
Cooma (NSW)	Port Macquarie (NSW)	
Dubbo (NSW)	Queanbeyan (NSW)	
Echuca (VIC)	Queenstown (TAS)	
Esperance (WA)	Renmark (SA)	
Geelong (VIC)	Rockhampton (QLD)	

Appendix K

Countries Australia has a Tax Treaty with:

Argentina	Ireland	Singapore
Austria	Italy	Slovakia
Belgium	Japan	South Africa
Canada	Kiribati	South Korea
Chile	Malaysia	Spain
China	Malta	Sri Lanka
Czech Republic	Mexico	Sweden
Denmark	Netherlands	Switzerland
Fiji	New Zealand	Taipei
Finland	Norway	Thailand
France	Papua New Guinea	Turkey
Germany	Philippines	United Kingdom
Hungary	Poland	United States
India	Romania	Vietnam
Indonesia	Russia	

Tax Secrets of a Real Estate Millionaire

About the author

Born in a small central Queensland town, Dymphna Boholt began her journey growing up on a cattle station in the Australian bush. Her first investment was an old milking cow named Blackie that was the impetus to fund her university degree in Accounting and Economics.

Upon graduation from the Australian National University in Canberra, Dymphna worked for the prestigious Coopers & Lybrand (one of the big eight at that time in accountancy firms worldwide). Her experience has spanned a variety of other roles both as financial controller, certified financial planner and consulting professional in the liquor, mining, manufacturing, stockbroking, banking and finance industries.

In 1994, she found herself 'starting over' after a divorce left her with very little money, pregnant and a toddler to support on her own. To get back on her feet, she moved to the Sunshine Coast, Queensland and focussed her attention on building her private client accounting business that she had been operating in conjunction with her other roles since she first got her tax agent license in 1986.

Keen to move away from the constraints of being a solo mum who was working full time, she decided to try her hand at real estate investment and focussed on properties that brought in more than they cost her. Within just one year she had accumulated a $3.5 million property portfolio, boasting $1.55 million in equity and more importantly, had totally replaced the accountancy income she was earning working a 40 – 60 hour week through passive real estate investments.

Today she has a multi-million dollar international property portfolio and is regarded as one of Australia's leading real estate strategists and educators, specialising in asset protection, taxation and investing, sharing her expansive knowledge through events, mentoring programs, and educational products.

The now happily remarried mother of three, lives on the beautiful Sunshine Coast of Queensland, Australia, on her 54 acre piece of paradise, completely surrounded by rainforest, birds, creeks and wildlife.

Dymphna's websites offer a comprehensive and growing range of free information, including articles, audios and other resources that can help you with your real estate investing, personal finance and business planning and management.

Some useful asset protection resources are included in this book, but there are even more (and the list is growing all the time) on Dymphna's websites.

On the websites, you can also browse my growing list of products in the Product Shop, and find out about any upcoming events Dymphna is hosting or speaking at – she could be coming to an area near you soon!

www.DymphnaBoholt.com
www.iloverealestate.tv

The Ultimate Real Estate Success Coaching Program
www.DymphnaBoholt.com

Ultimate Real Estate Success Coaching Program
CD's & Manuals
Here's how you can take your education to the next level and get 12-months of coaching by Dymphna Boholt. This program includes 4 critical parts to real estate investing success. They are Cash Flow, Capital Growth, Tax Minimisation and Asset Protection.

In this program, you receive the A to Z library of real estate investing as well as live training and monthly coaching calls. Here's a list of what you get...

Create Passive Income through Real Estate Cashcows Home Self-Study Course
9 CD's, Audio & Workbook
If it's just positive cashflow real estate you're looking for – then this is the perfect program for you, where I reveal how you can find real estate cashcows that could quite possibly within 12 months, replace your current income.

How to Legally Reduce Your Tax without Losing Any Money Home Self-Study Course
2 CD's, Audio & Workbook
It's no secret that the greatest wealth killer of our society today is the amount of money that the governments take from you. Learn how to turn the tables on the government… legally.

Safe as a Bomb-Shelter Asset Protection Secrets Home Self-Study Course
2 CD's, Audio & Workbook
It's often been said that making money is easy. It's keeping it that is the problem. Many wealthy people have experienced this first-hand

and have had to build their fortunes many times over. Learn how the rich legally protect themselves their assets.

Instant Growth Real Estate Accelerator System Home Self-Study Course
4 CD's, Audio & Workbook
You'll get an insider look of how I've been able to not only create positive income, but also grow my portfolio without the constraints that most investors experience with other people's systems.

How to Turn Debt into Investment Dollars Home Self Study Course
5 CD's, Audio & Workbook
The fast effective way of turning debt into; dollars saved, dollars invested, dollars earning passive income.

Introduction to Investment Finance Home Self-Study Course
2 CD's, Audio & Workbook
In this financing manual we will try to break down the barriers between you, the house owner/investor and the banking/financing industry. We will give you an insight to how the banks look at you and your loans and try to give you an understanding of how they think.

Ultimate Property Bootcamp Home Self-Study Course
10 DVD's & Slide Book
You'll get a massive 300 page manual with 10 DVD's from my recent Ultimate Real Estate Seminar, where I reveal my secret formula that enabled me to replace my
income with cashflow from real estate.

The Ultimate Real Estate 3-Day LIVE Training Event
Live Event for a list of the up and coming events.
Series Teleseminar Coaching Calls over a 12 month period. Once a month, we get together and build a platform for you to create amazing success fast. You'll have the opportunity to interact with me, ask questions on the call and clear up any doubt that you can do this.

Tax Secrets of a Real Estate Millionaire

Other publications by Dymphna Boholt...

Confessions of a Real Estate Millionaire
by Dymphna Boholt

This is an amazing journey and a rollercoaster ride of real emotions. Real estate millionaires are not all created equal. If making money in real estate was all about strategy and tactics, surely there would be a lot more of them around? Dymphna Boholt not only delivers you the appropriate skills required to achieve real estate wealth and success, she goes deep into the mind, the heart and emotion that all millionaires go through.

You don't become a real estate millionaire overnight, however, the decision to do so can be made in a heartbeat. Dymphna Boholt shows you the path that she took and how her path has motivated others to follow a similar journey to the ultimate dream and freedom of living off passive income created through real estate.

Packed with useful tips, techniques and advice, *Confessions of a Real Estate Millionaire* is a must read for anyone who wants to claim back their birthright and live a life on their own terms. Not only will you discover a system for wealth, you will also discover how to break through your current barriers and obstacles.

Tax Secrets of a Real Estate Millionaire
by Dymphna Boholt

Dymphna specifically goes through how to use real estate to leverage your wealth faster than you ever thought possible. Dymphna reveals specific strategies designed to maximise your income. Not only via cash flow and growth, but the often-overlooked area of efficient tax management.

It's no secret that the greatest wealth killer of our society today is the amount of money that the governments take from you... and the sad fact is that most people allow this to happen with very little knowledge or skill of how to turn the tables on the government... legally.

If you want to be a successful real estate investor, then you must understand how to take advantage of the Tax Act and make it work for you rather than you working for it.

Tax Secrets of a Real Estate Millionaire

101 Top Ten Tips of a Real Estate Millionaire
by Dymphna Boholt

In this book, Dymphna Boholt collates her Top Ten Tips for 101 real estate related topics. Covering everything from mindset, preparation and questions to ask when assembling your team, right through to taxation and asset protection, as well as all processes involved in the development of your successful real estate portfolio.

Packed with useful tips, hints and advice, *101 Top Ten Tips of a Real Estate Millionaire* will be your 'go to' handbook for all things real estate.

Books are available at all good book stores or are available online at:

www.DymphnaBoholt.com

SPECIAL GIFT

Free Offer and Resources from Dymphna Boholt

Congratulations! You've come a long way already. If you've read this far then you have distinguished yourself from the rest of the pack and elevated your potential to join the top 5% of the wealth builders on this planet.

I'd like to reward you with ongoing education and free resources so you can continue the momentum that this book has created for you. The value of these resources is well over $985.

Gift #1: The Ultimate 1 Day Real Estate Success Seminar. Spend a whole day with me and I will reveal to you my unique real estate secrets quadrant which is protect, maximise, wealth, cash flow. Some teach one or two of the secrets but nobody teaches all four and how important they are in growing your wealth fast.
Value $495, Yours Free!

Gift #2: Bring a second person to Ultimate Real Estate Secrets event for free.
Value $295, Yours Free!

Gift #3: Online audio newsletter, The Property Prophet Report. Every week I keep you updated with my audio newsletter. The property market is always changing, get the inside knowledge and the unfair advantage on how to capitalise, regardless of the economic climate.
Value $195, Yours Free!

To qualify for the bonuses, you need to register at the following exclusive link:

http://realestatesuccess.com.au/985bonus